Very good

This book belong to

„   "

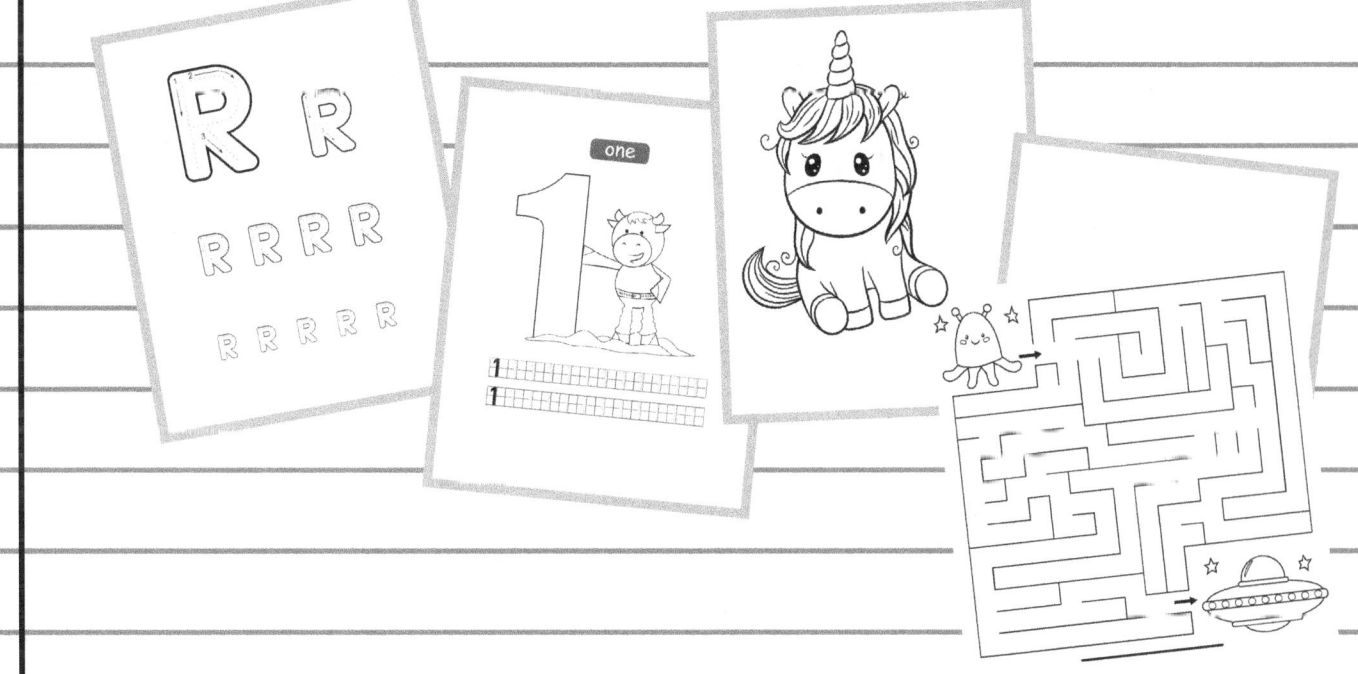

Keep working on it. You're improving

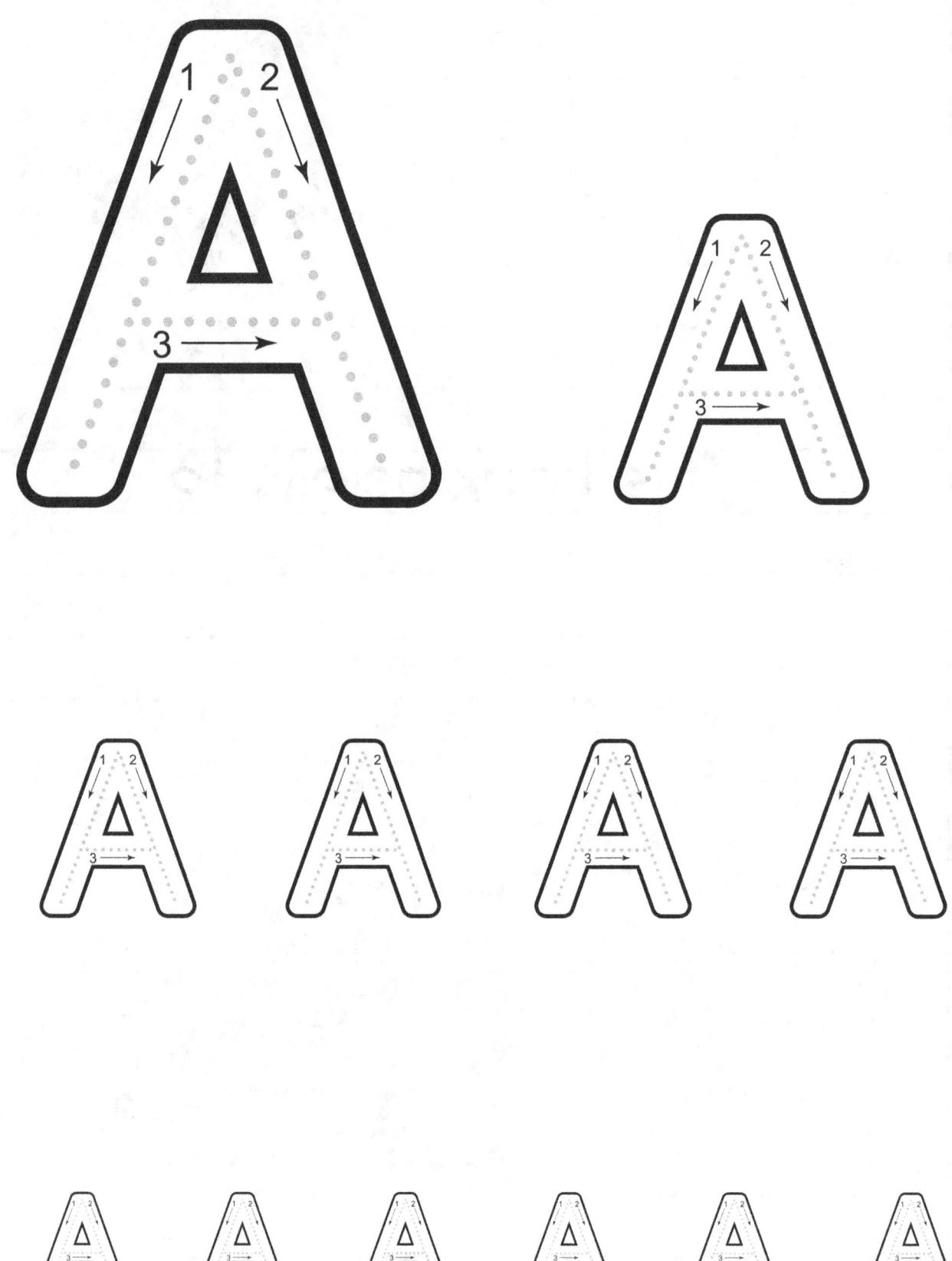

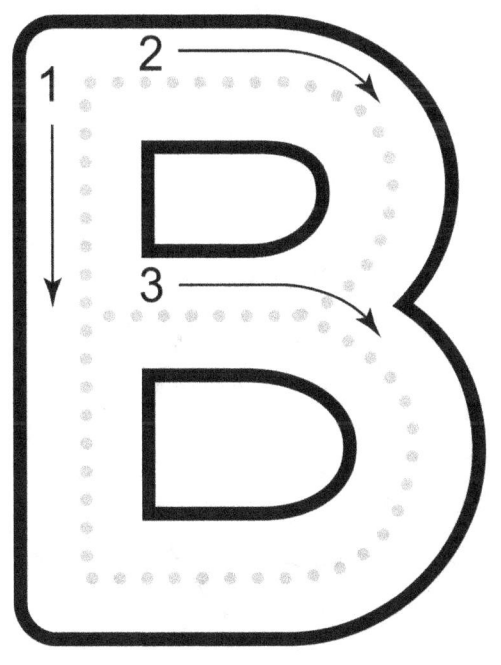
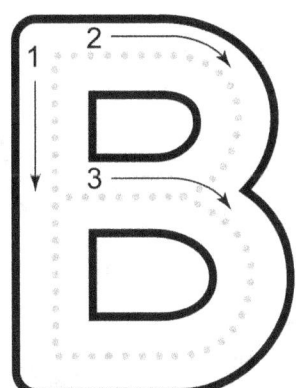
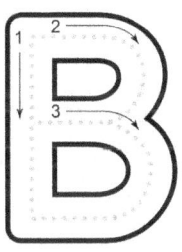
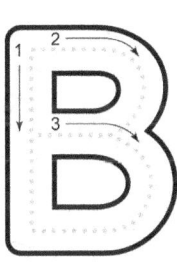
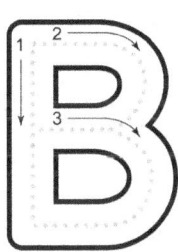
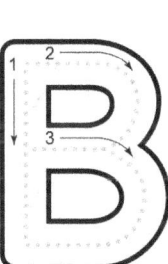
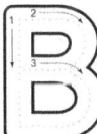
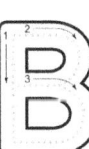
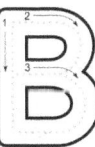
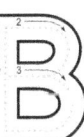
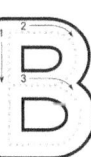
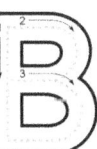

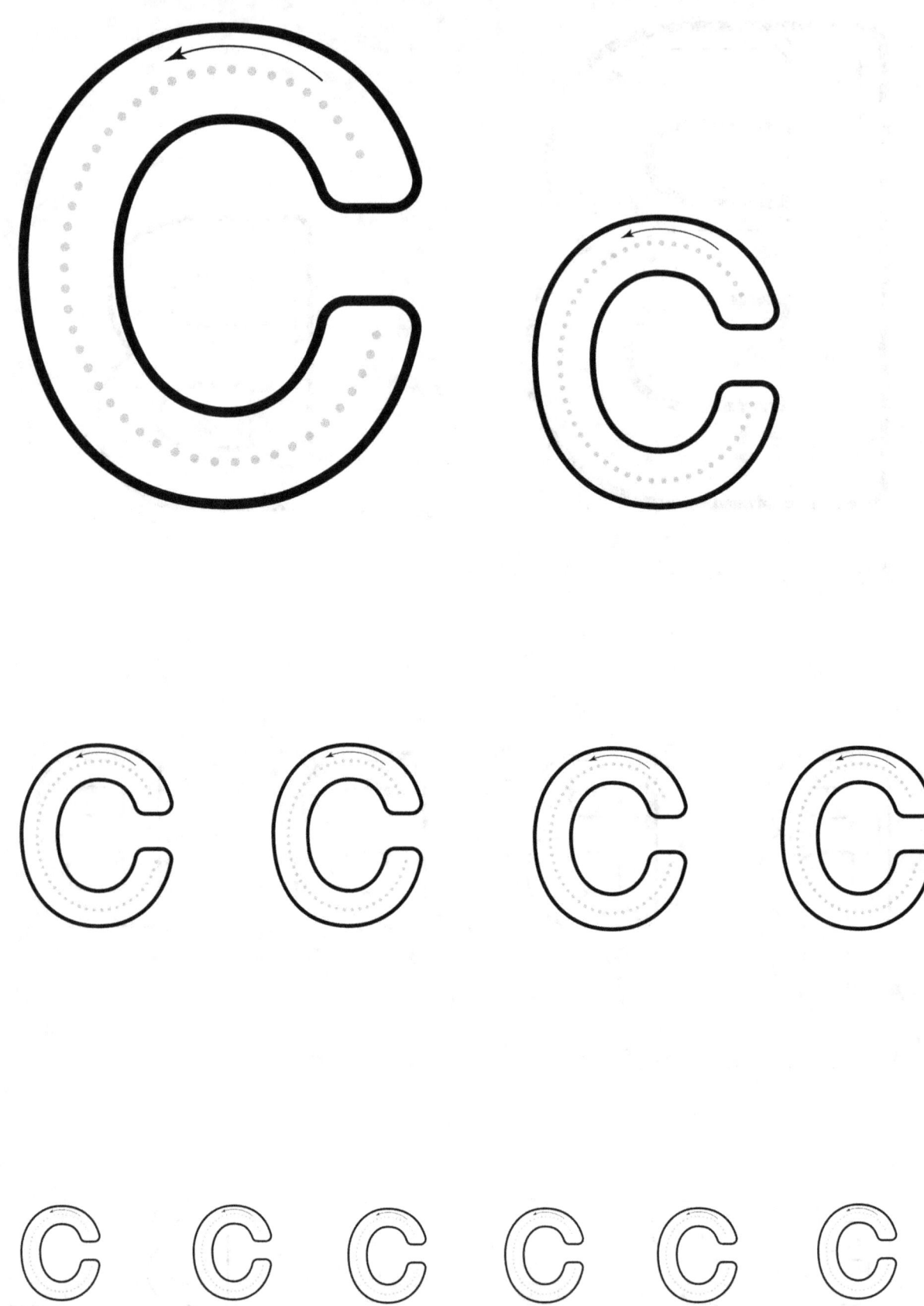

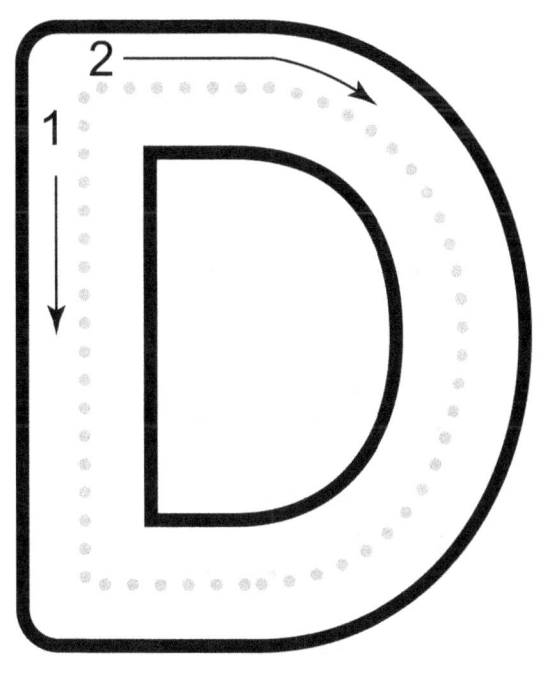
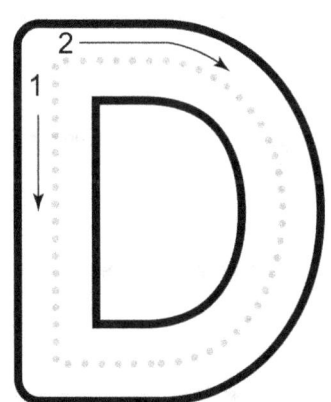
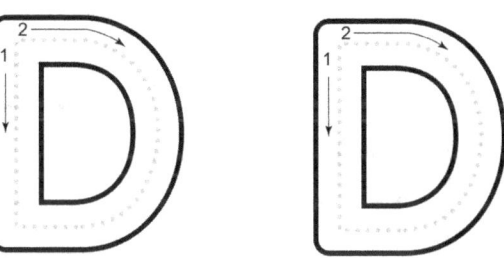
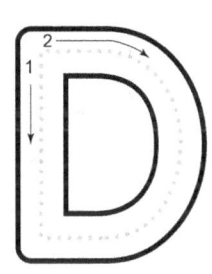
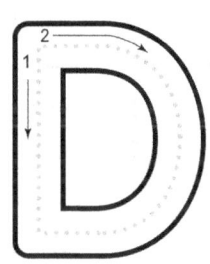

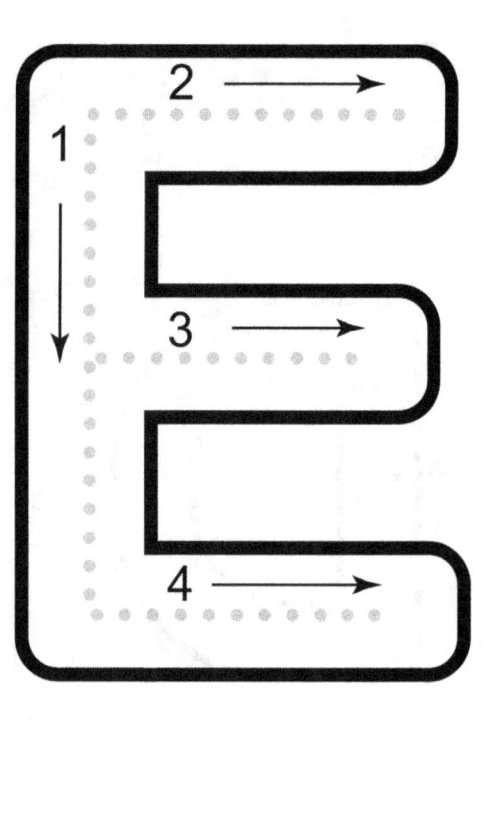
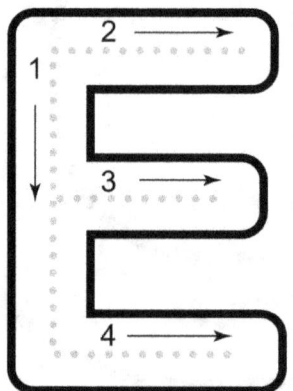

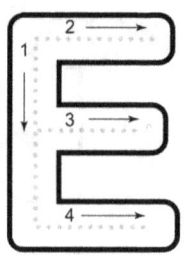
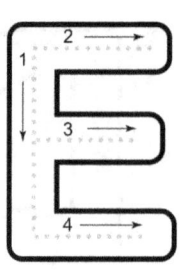
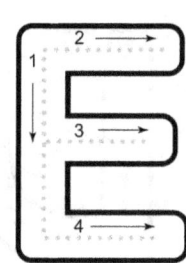
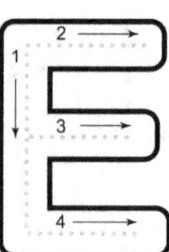

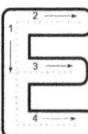
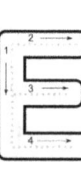
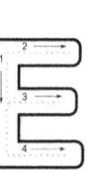
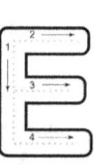
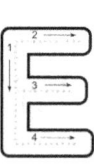
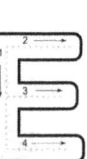

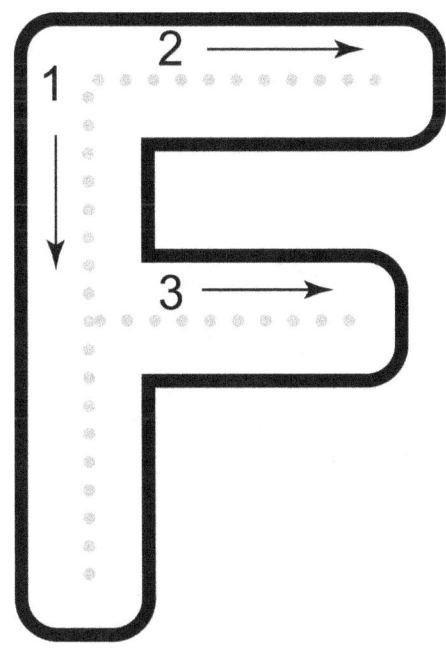
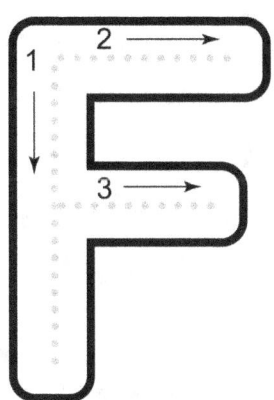
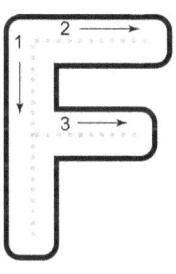
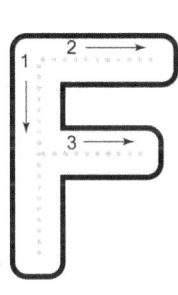
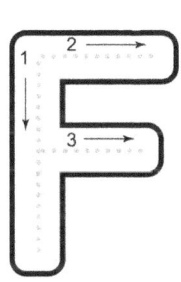
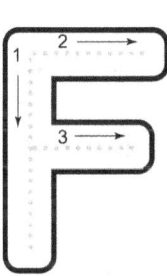
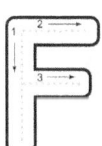
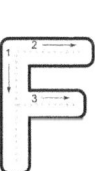
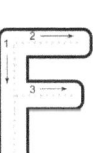
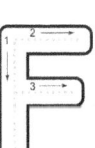
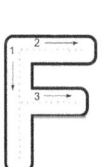
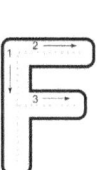

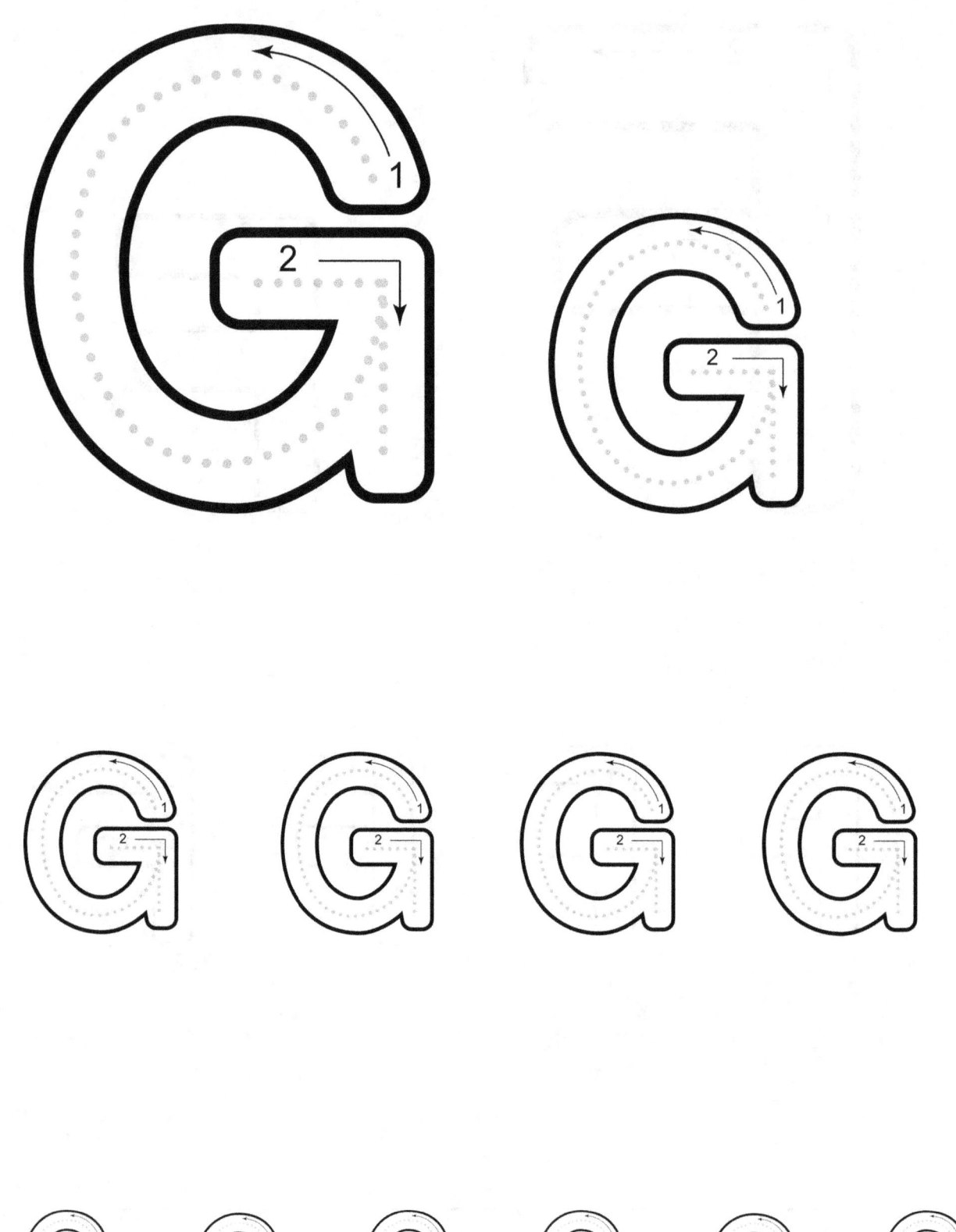

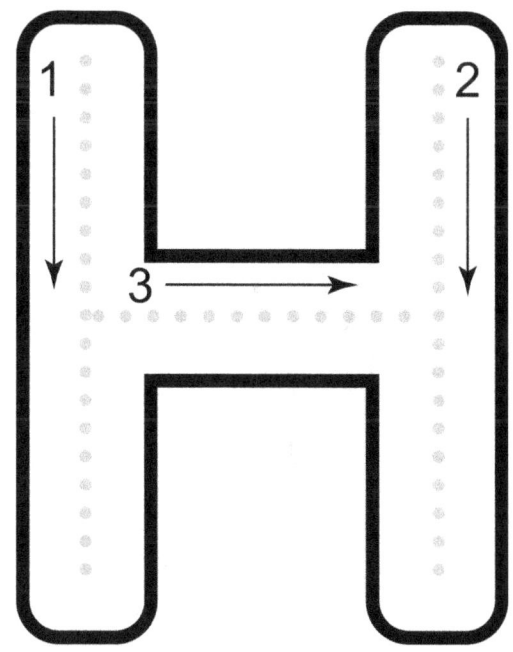
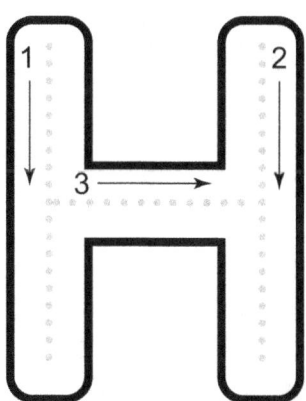

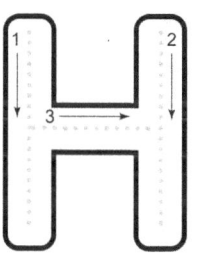
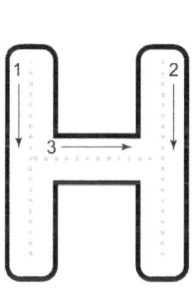
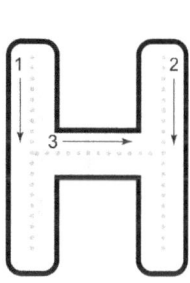
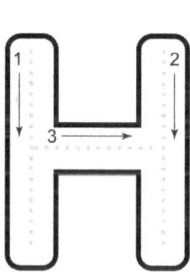

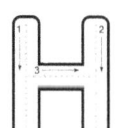
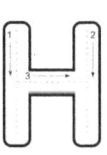
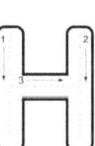
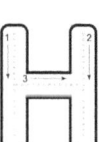
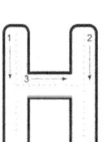
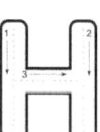

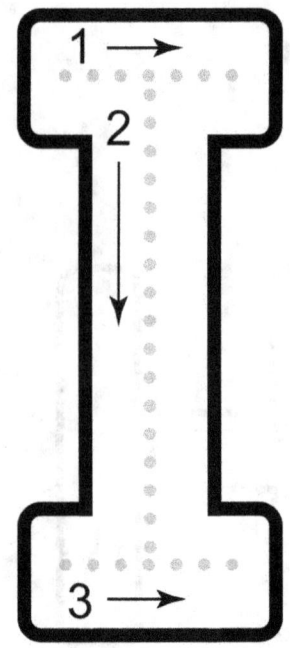
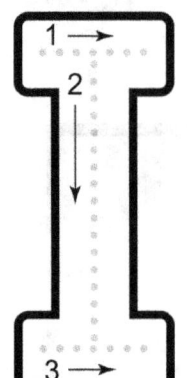
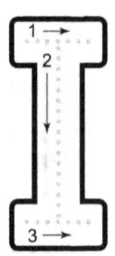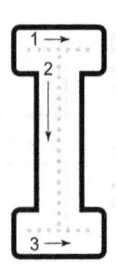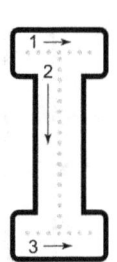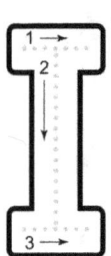
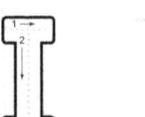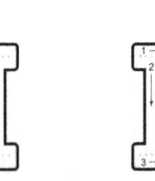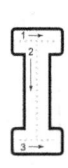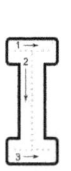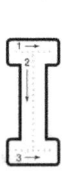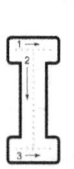

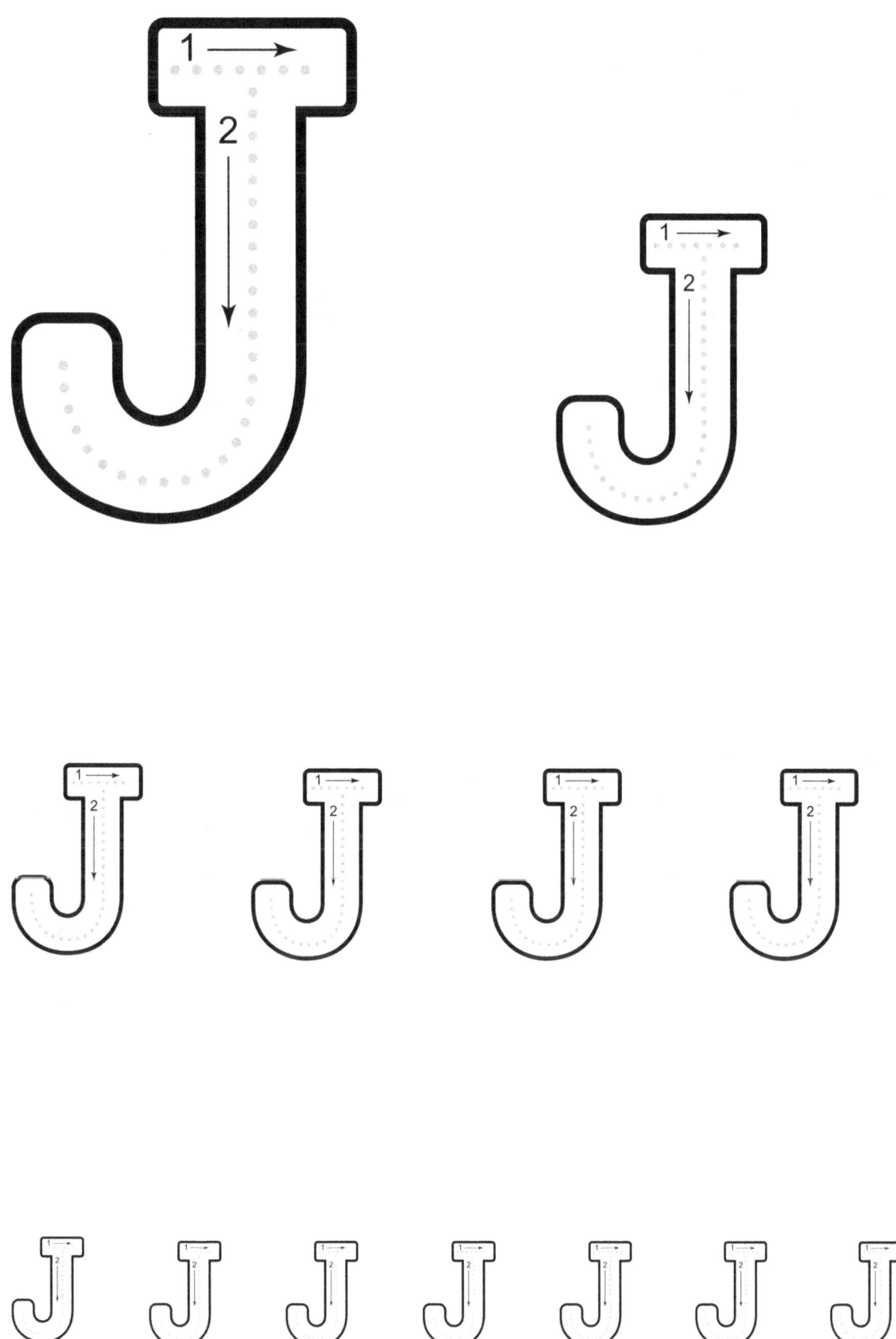

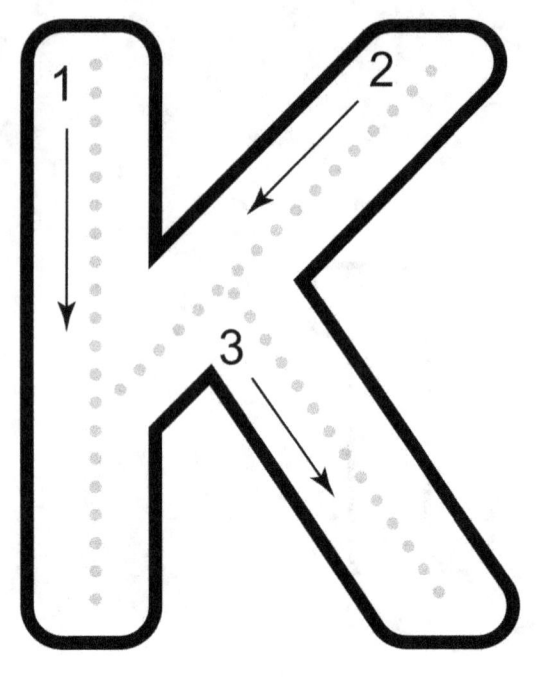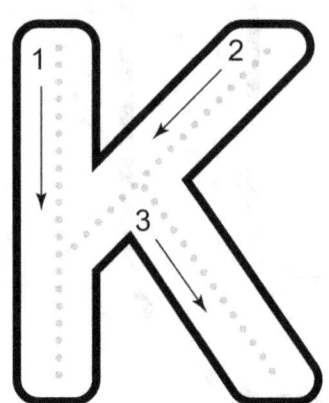

K K K K K

K K K K K

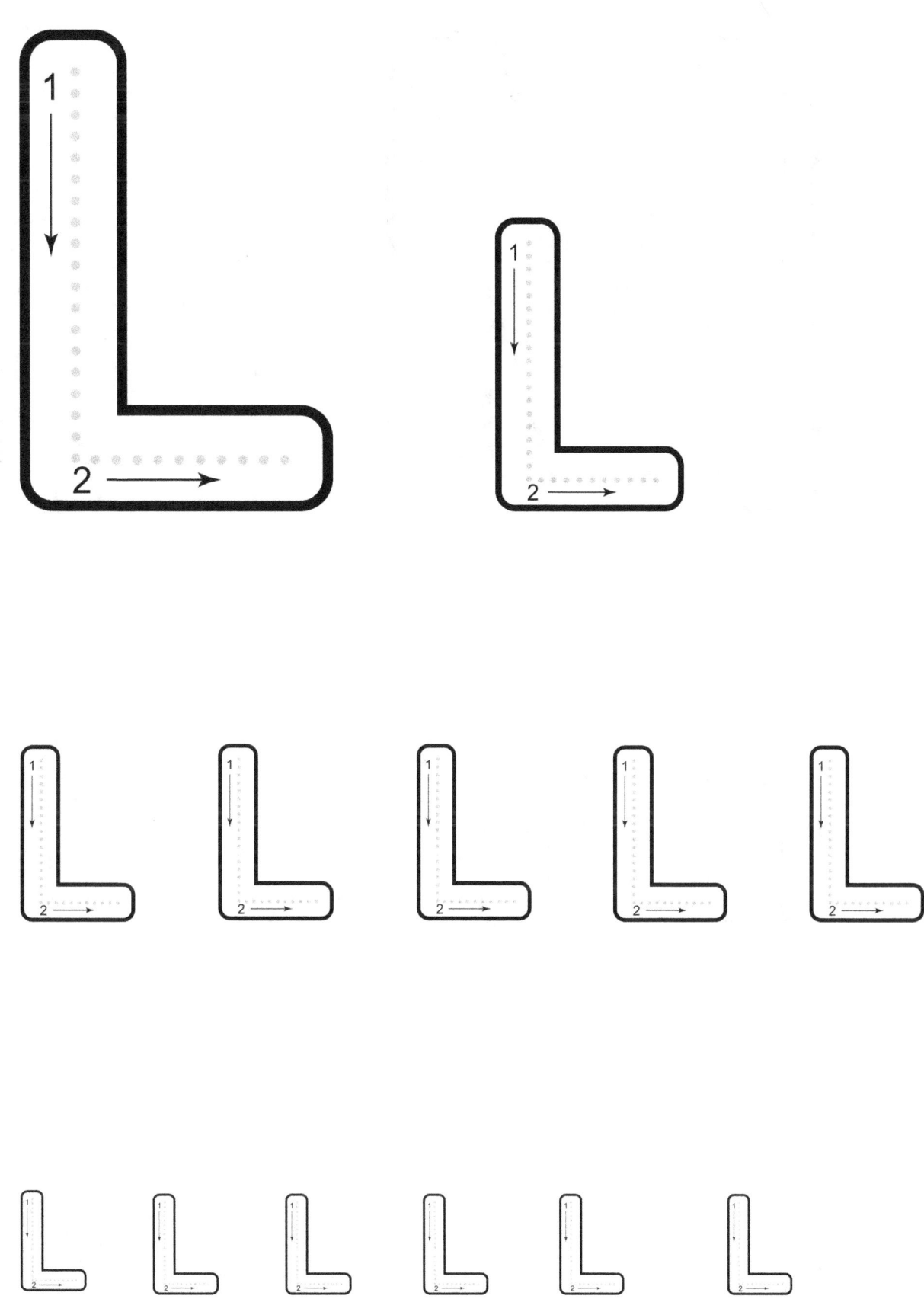

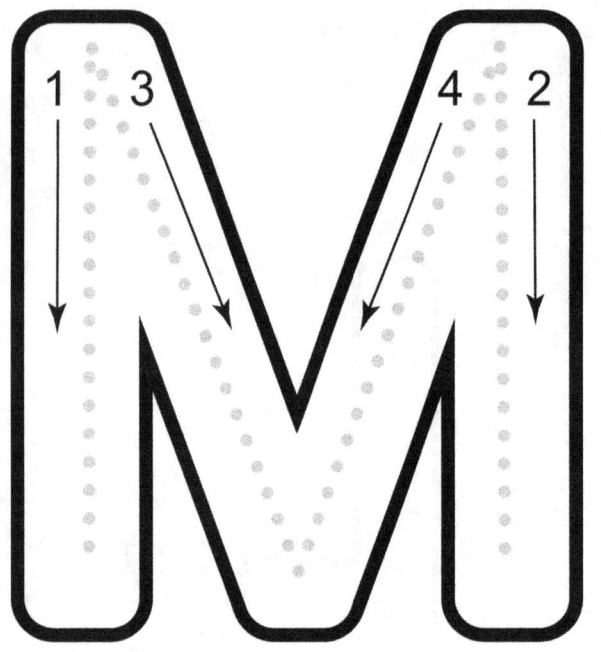
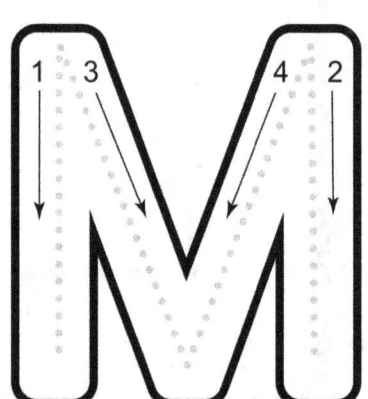
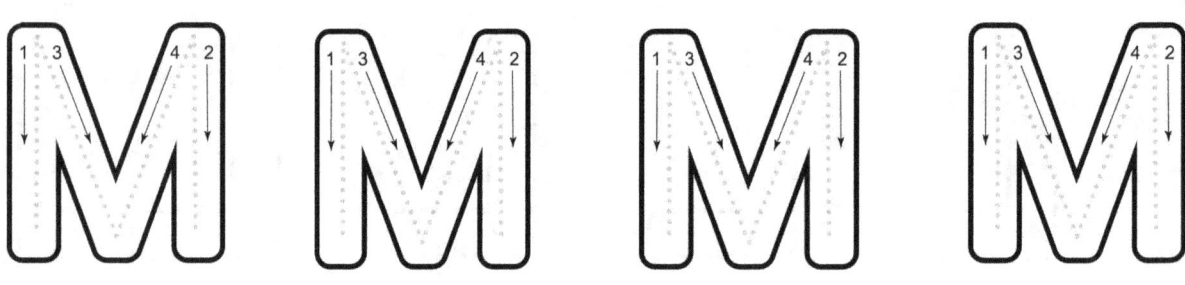

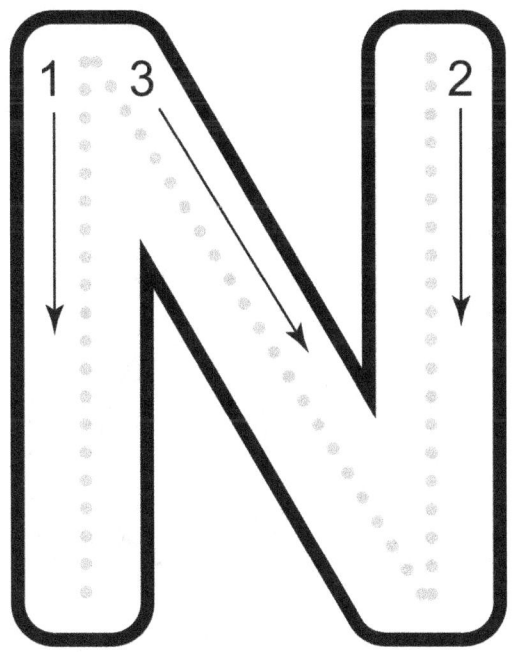
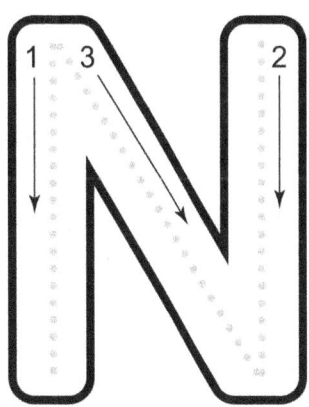
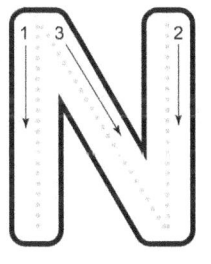
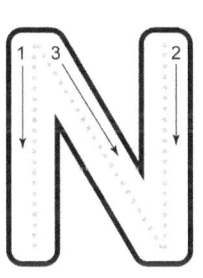
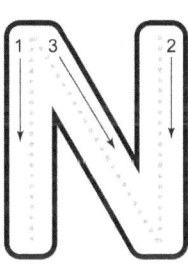
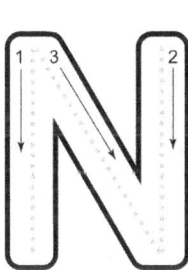

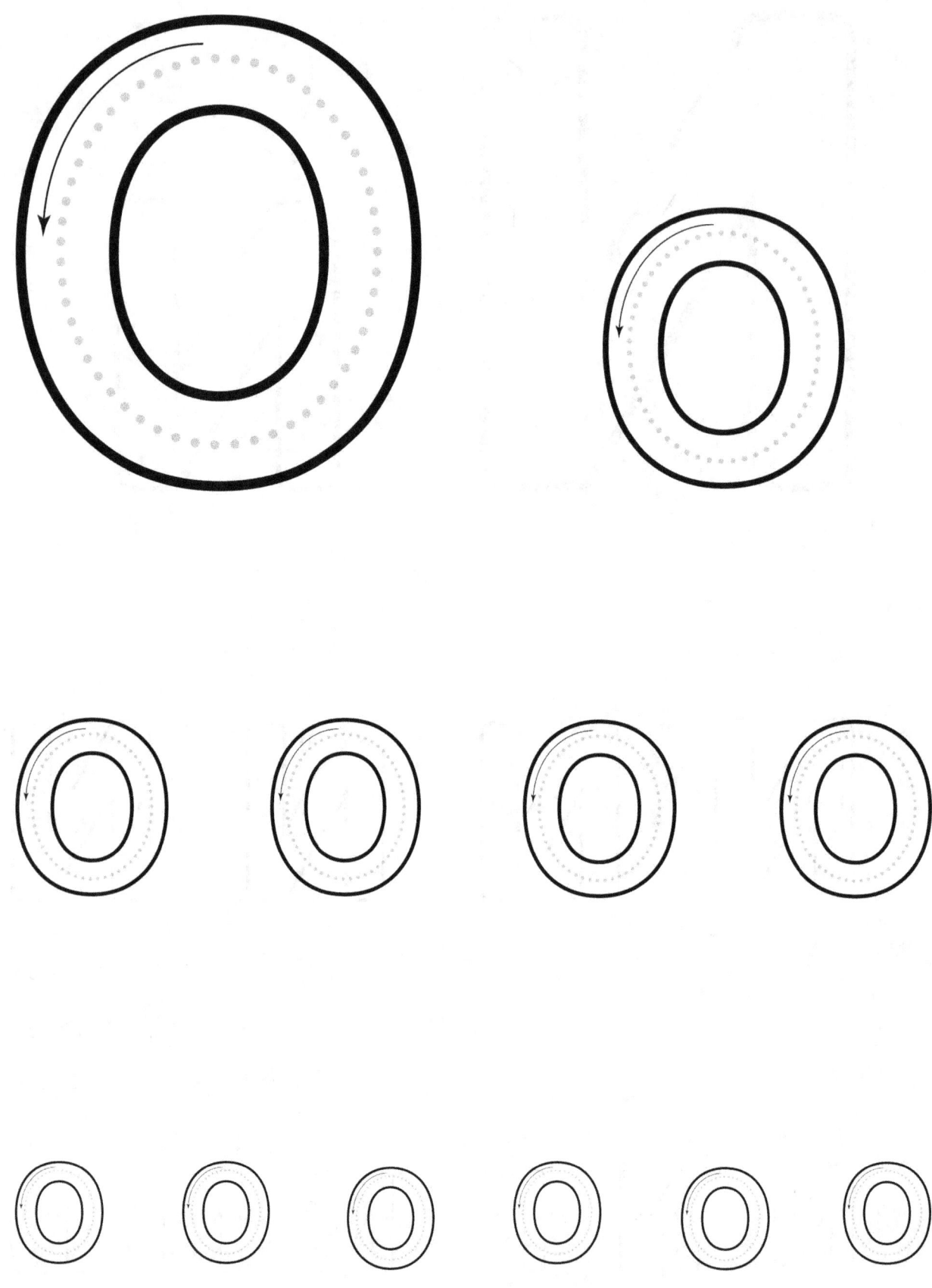

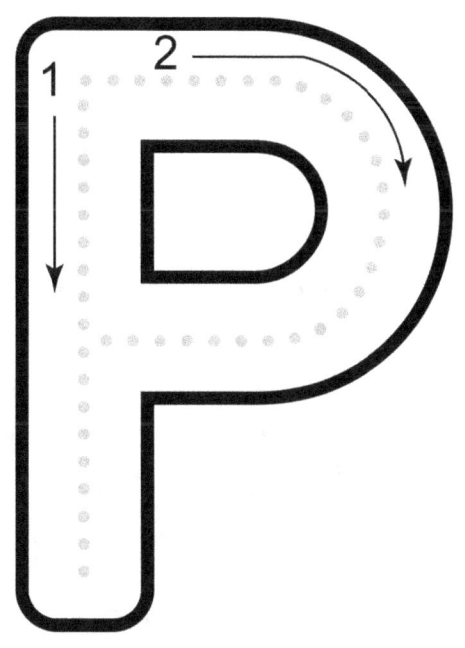
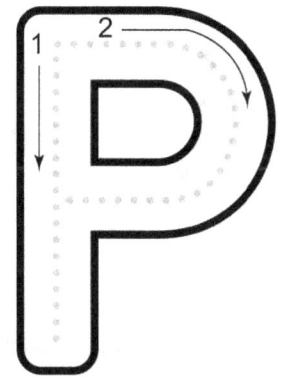
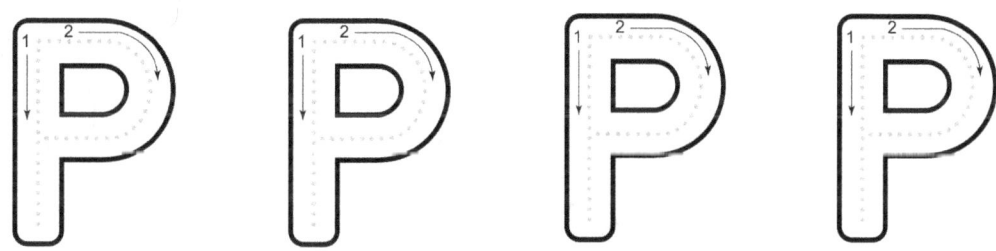
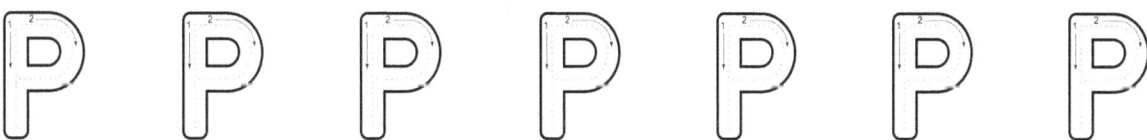

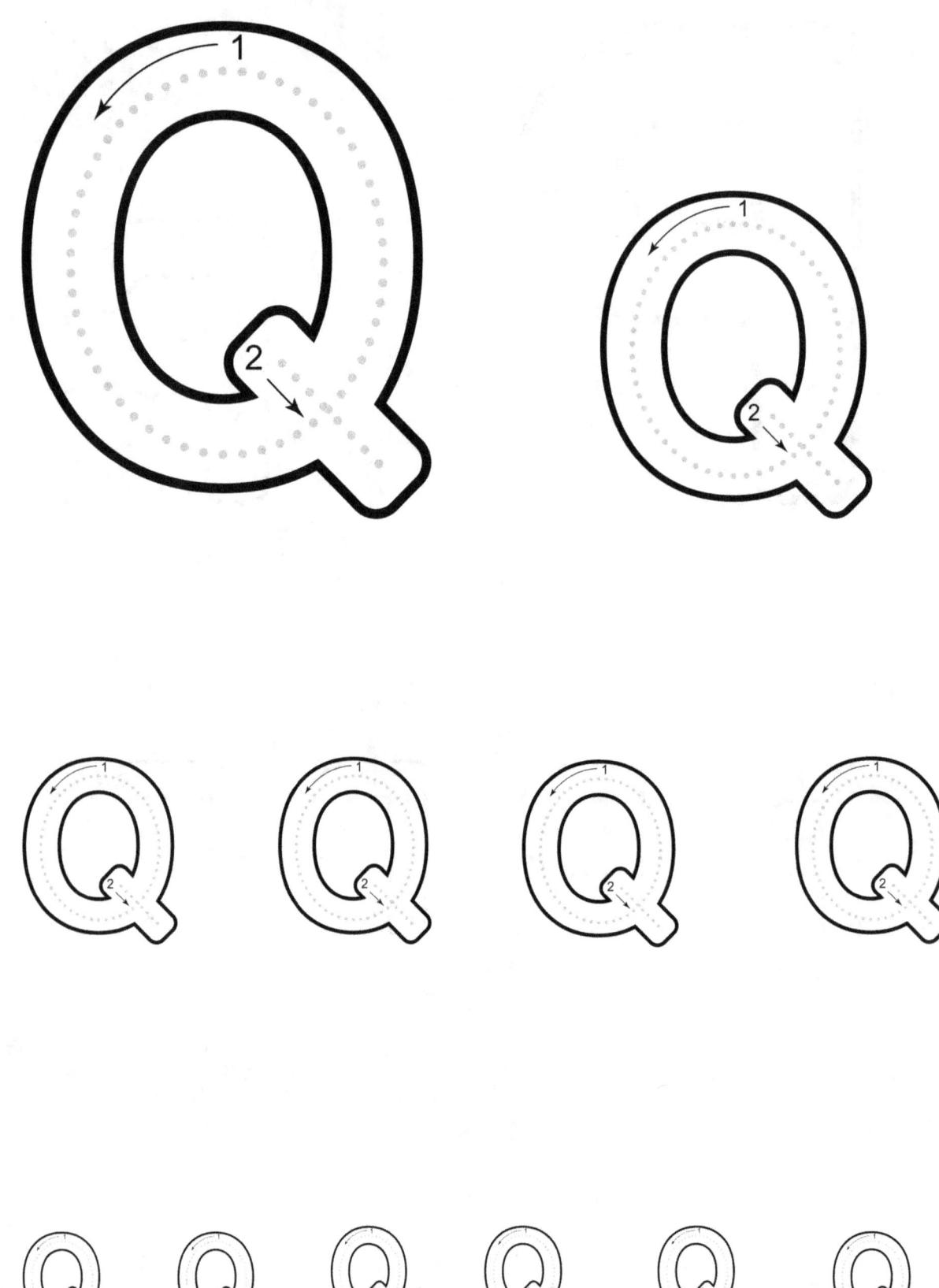

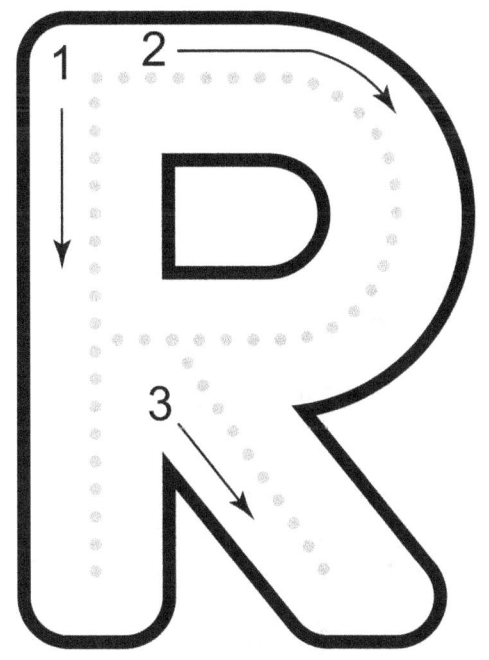
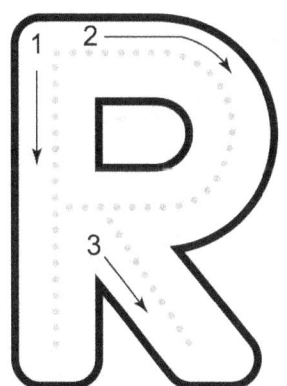

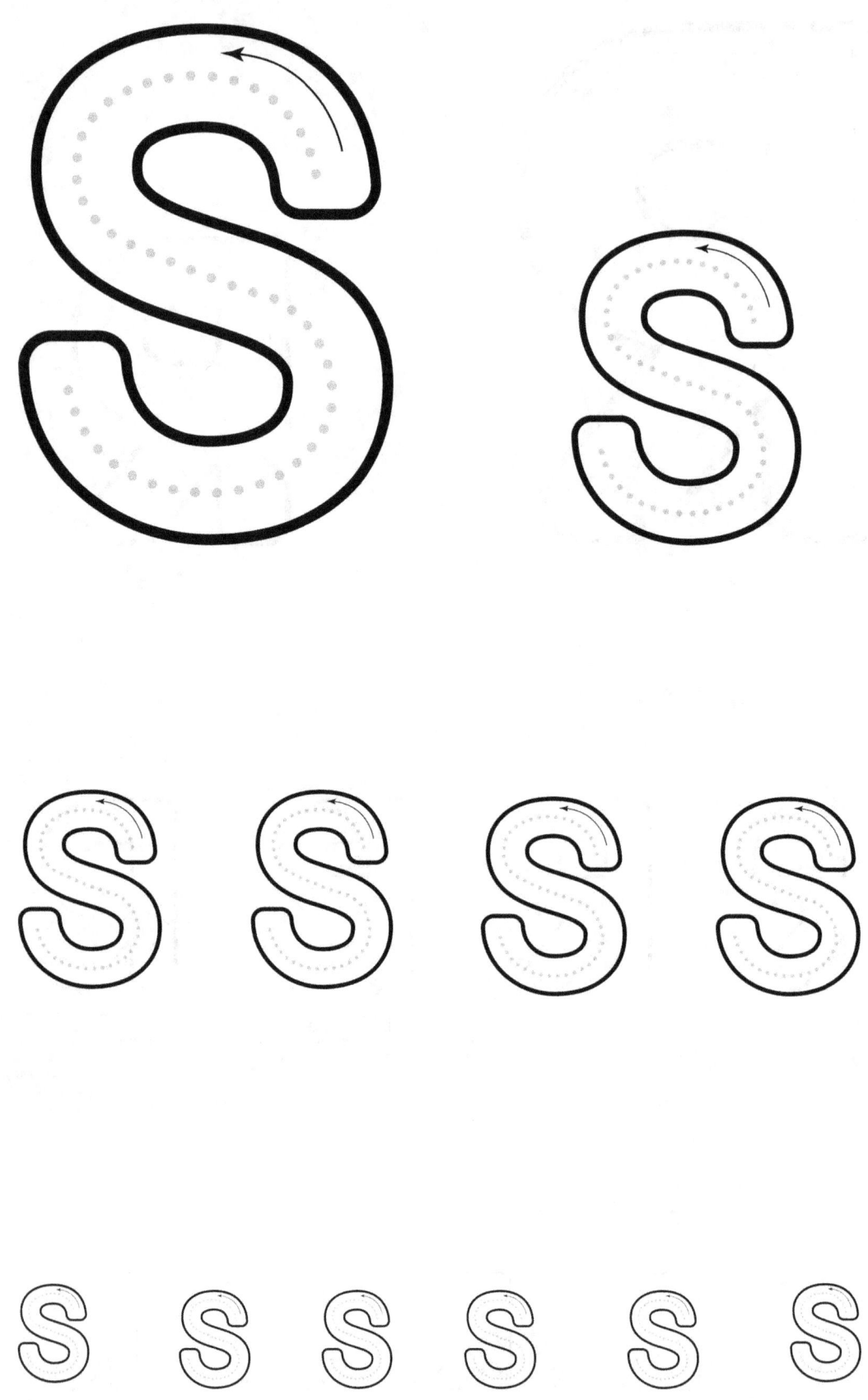

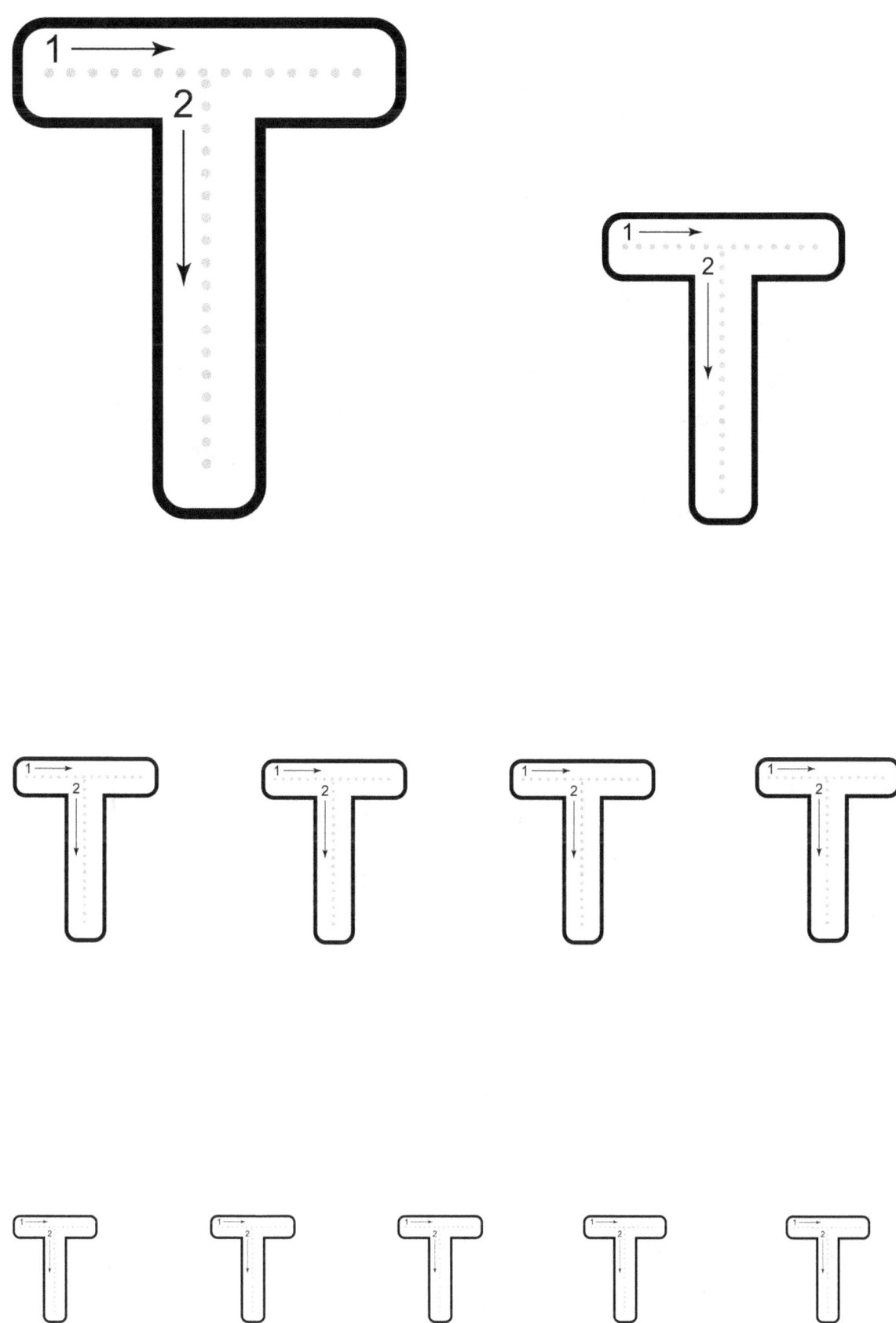

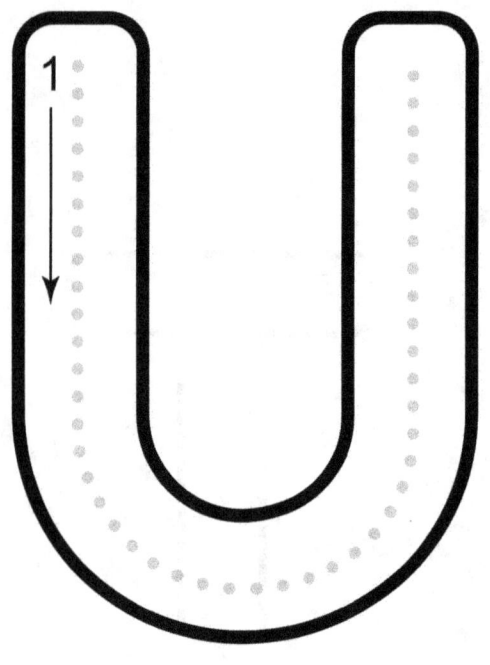
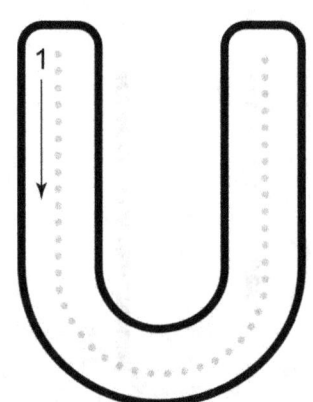
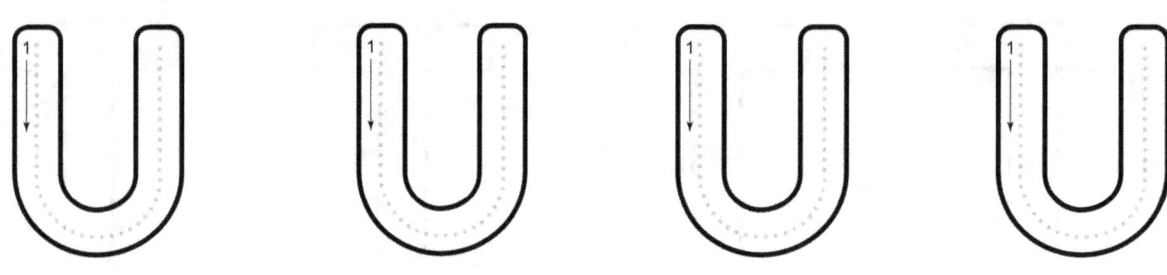

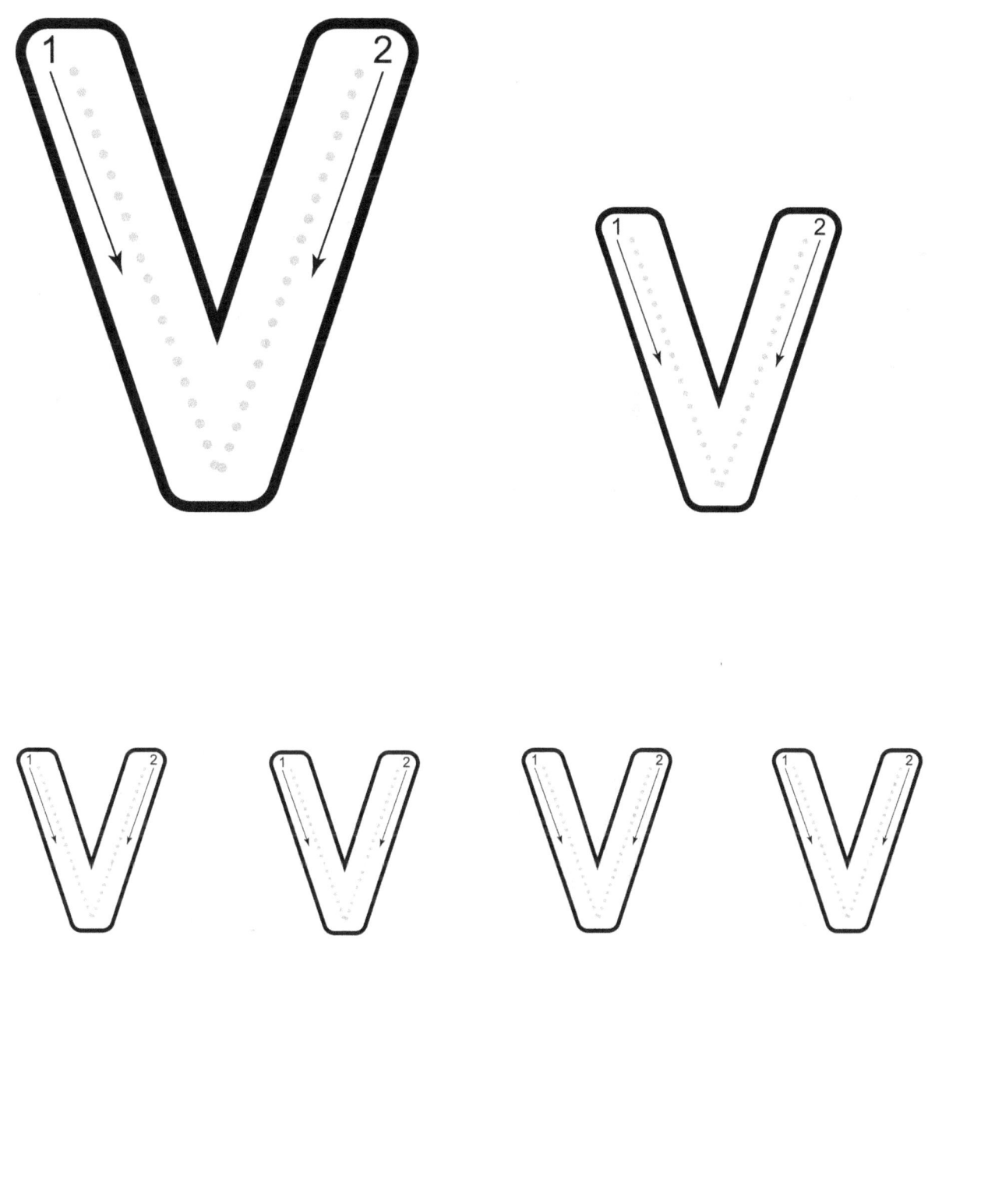

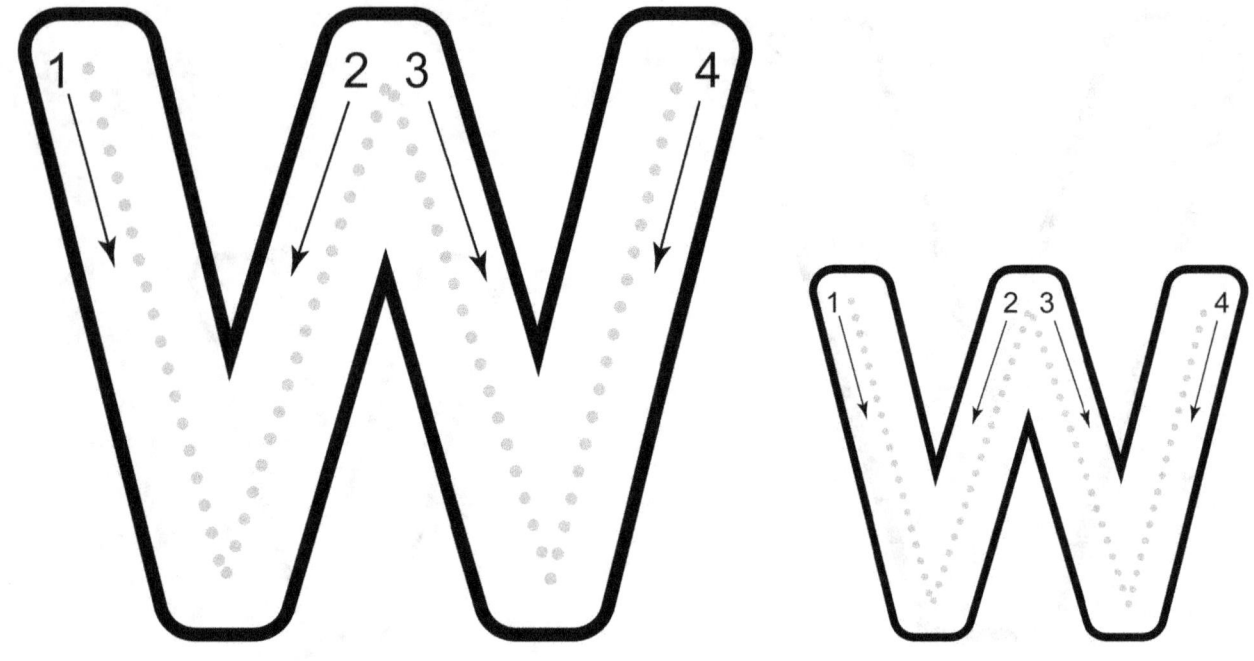

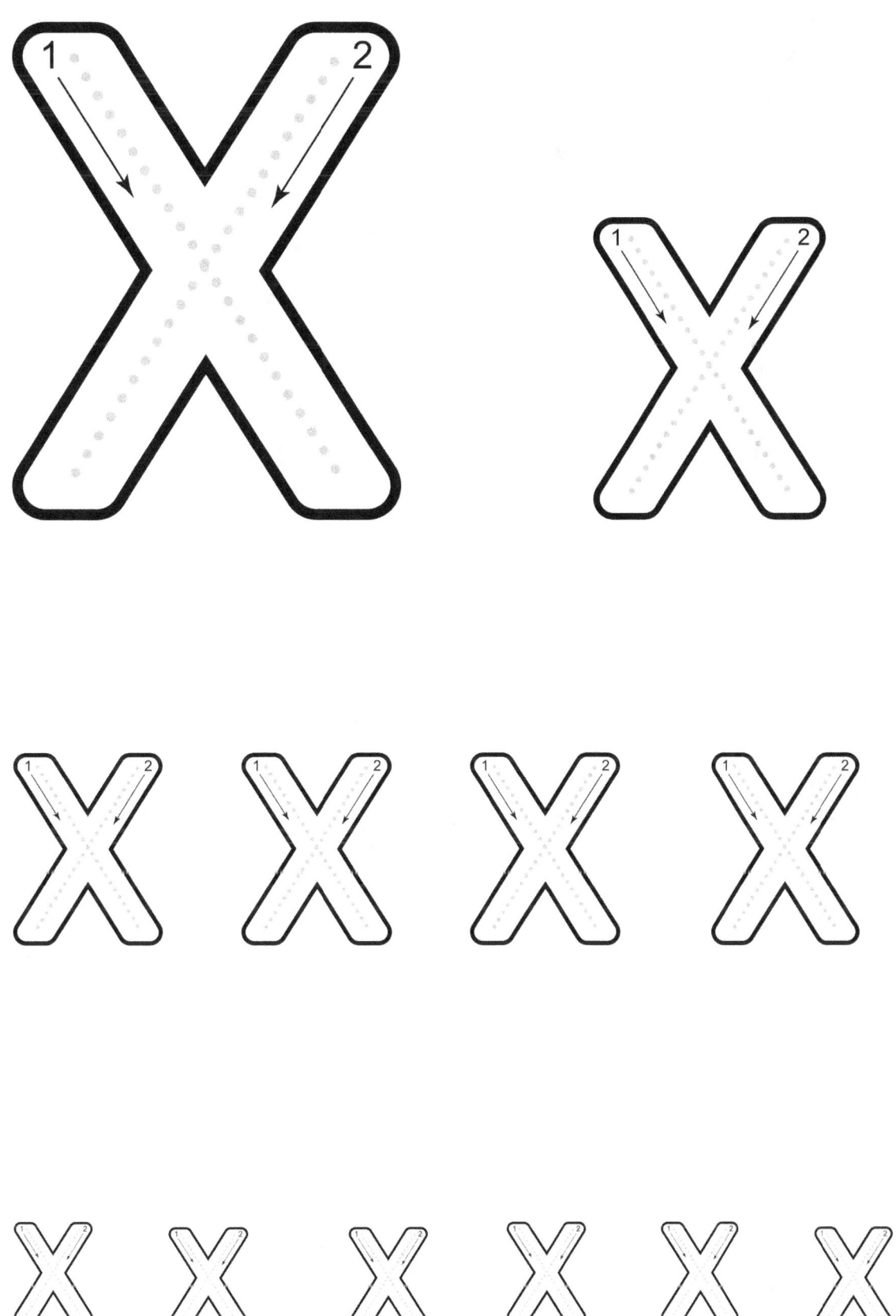

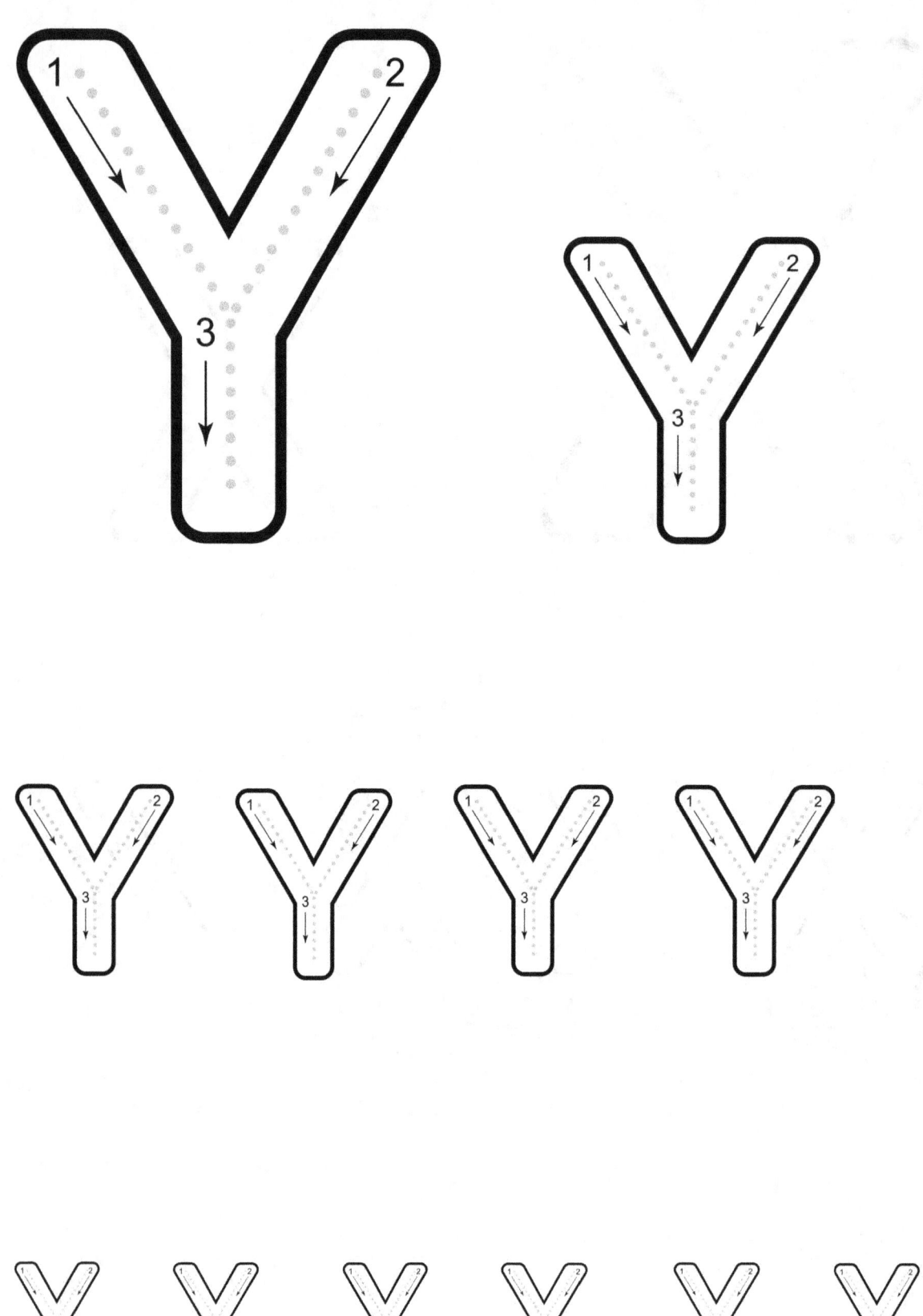

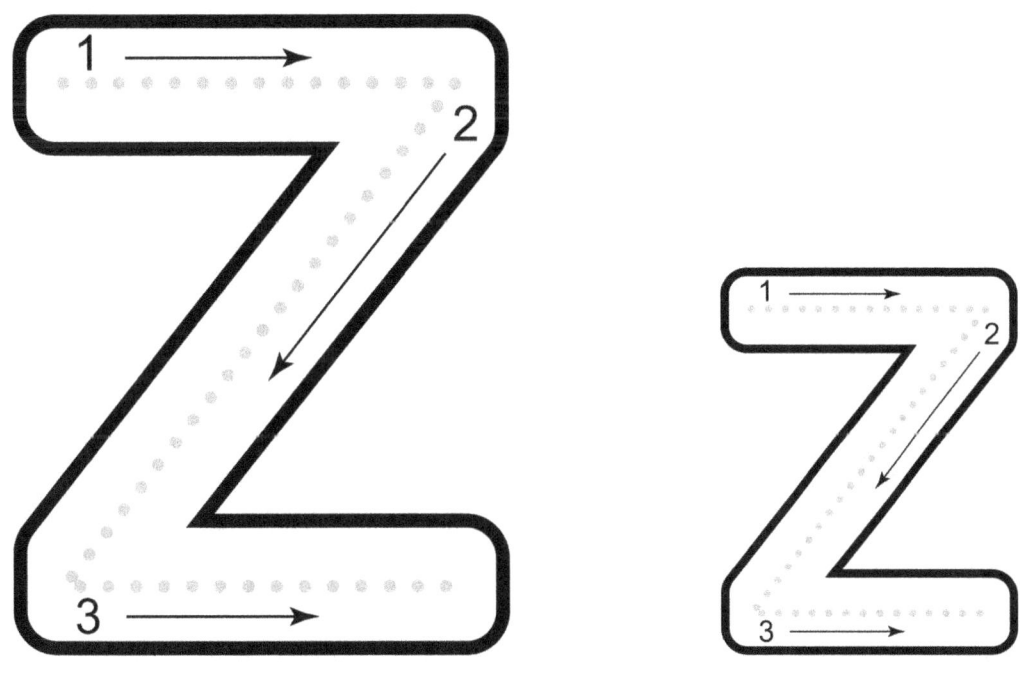

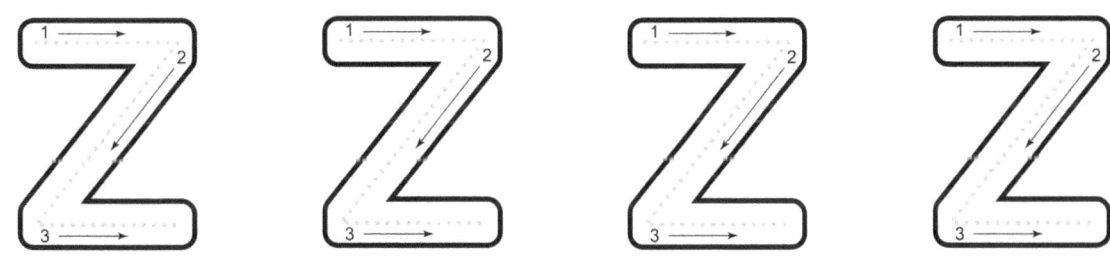

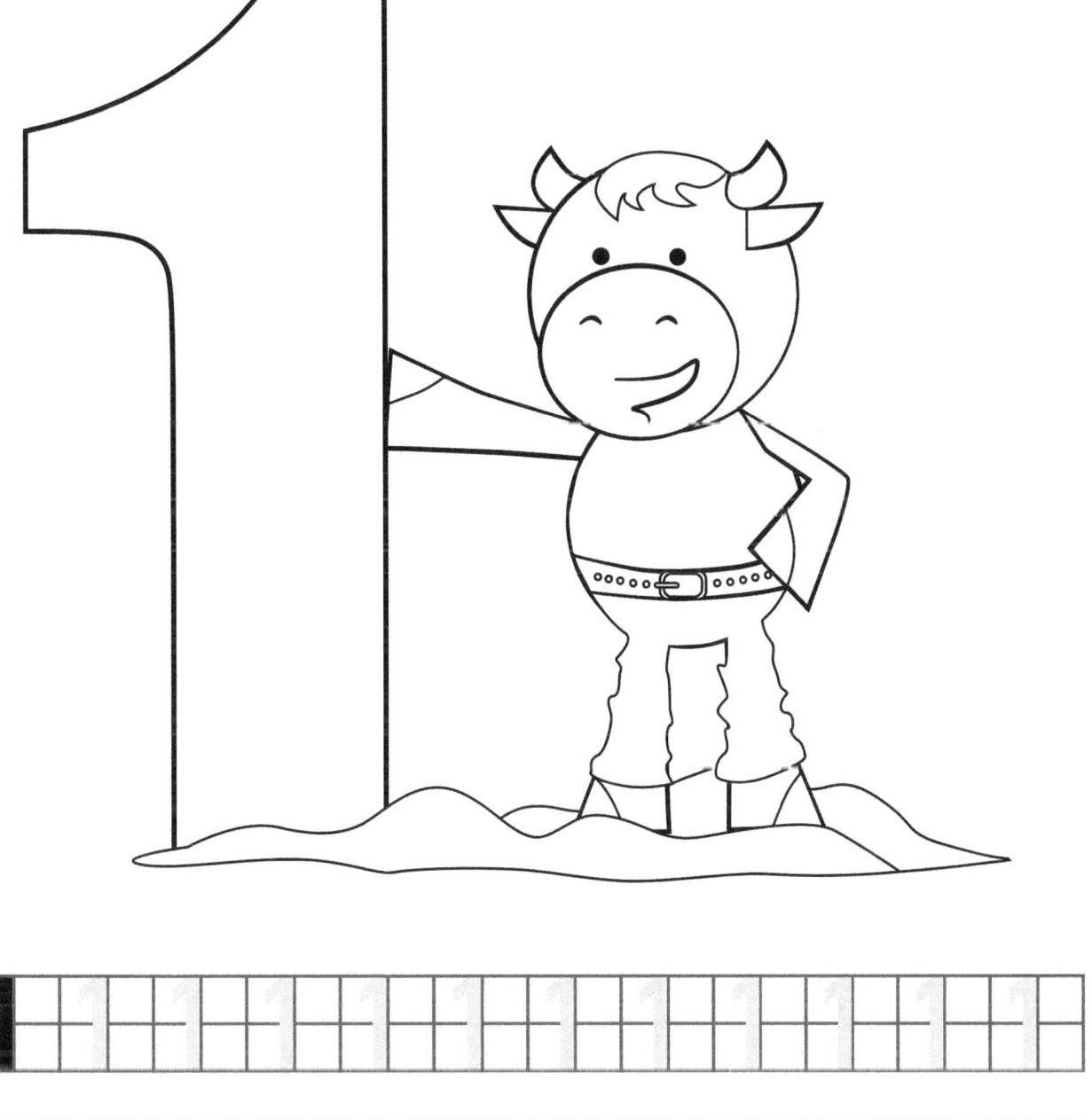

TWO

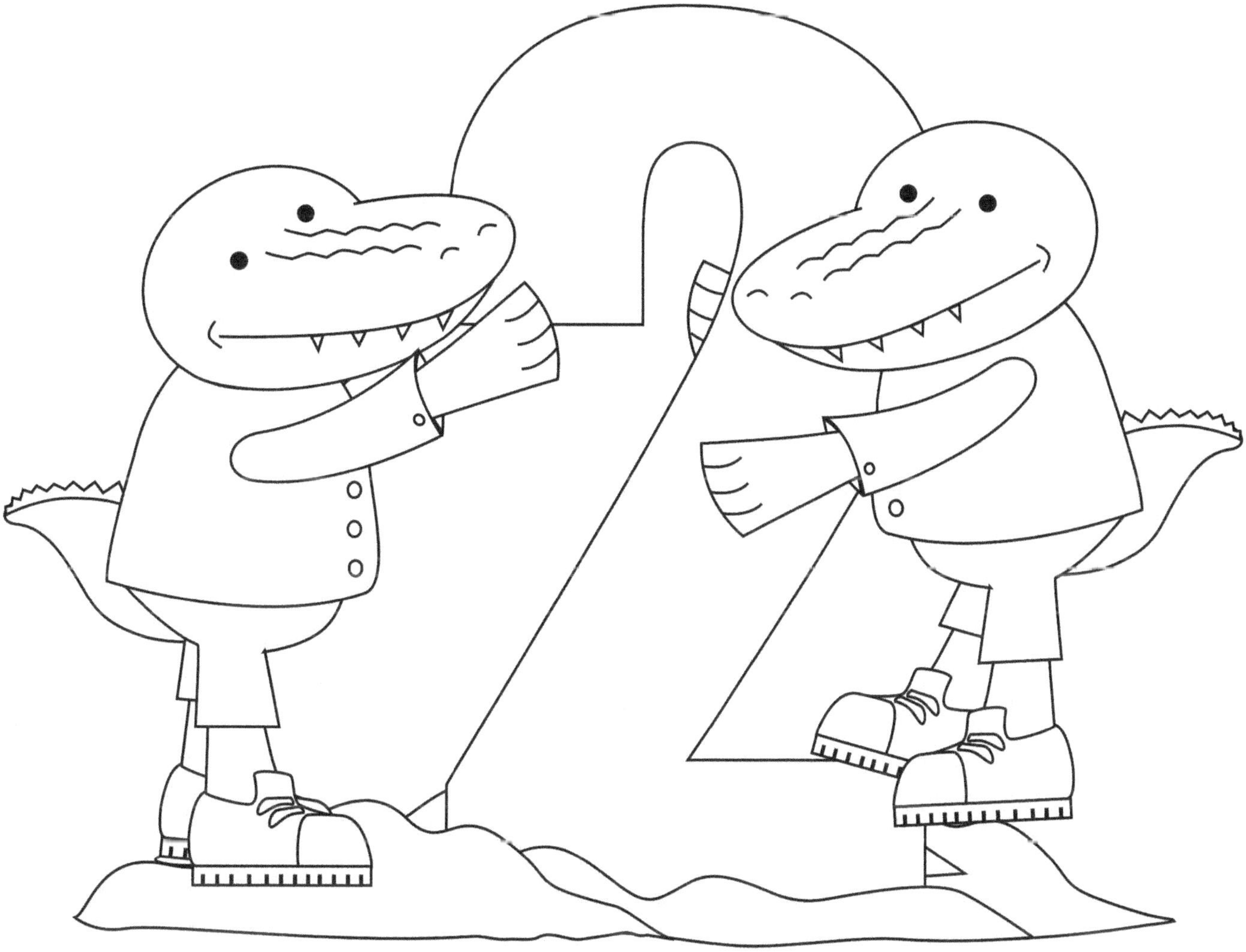

THREE

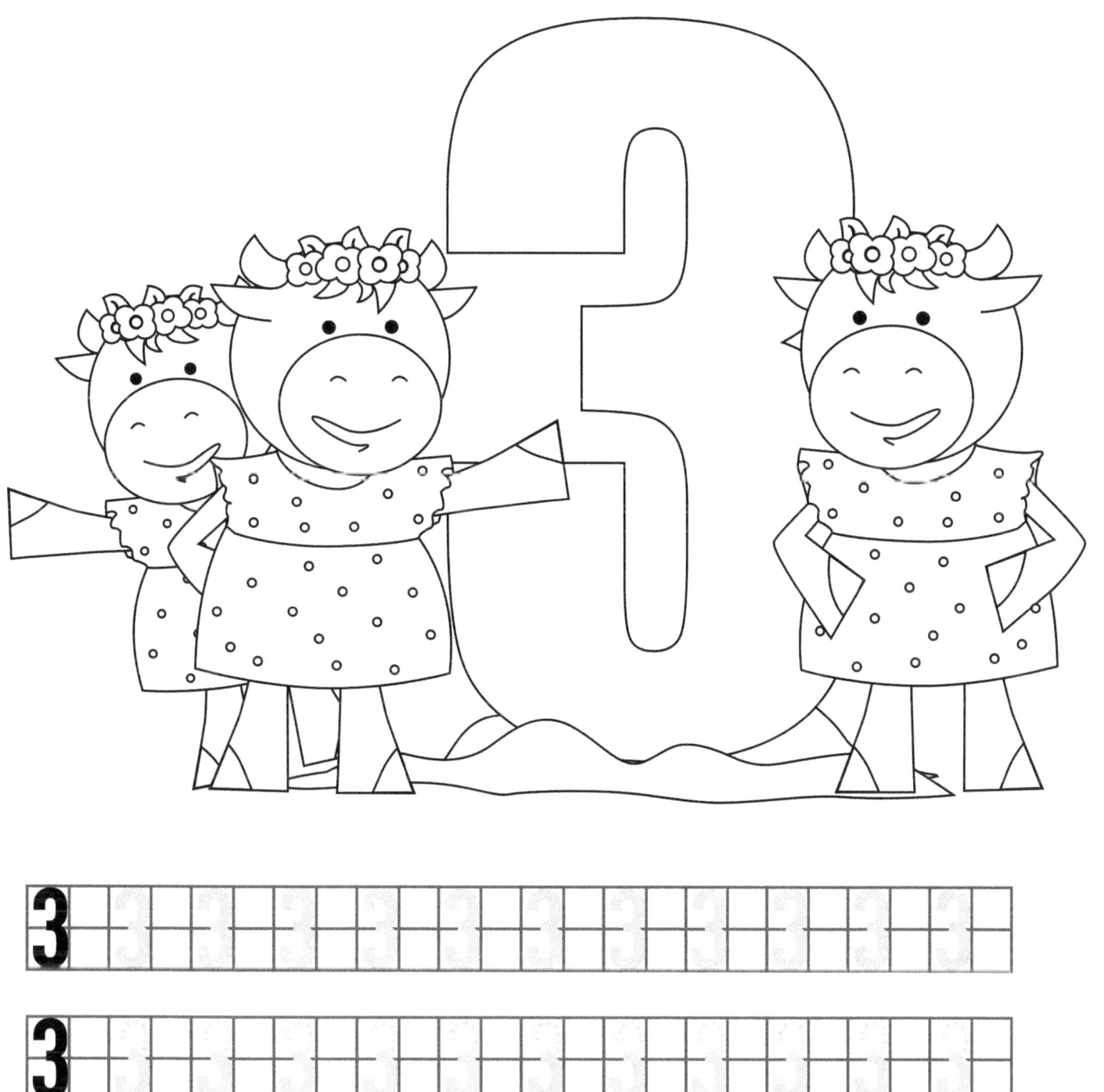

3
3

FOUR

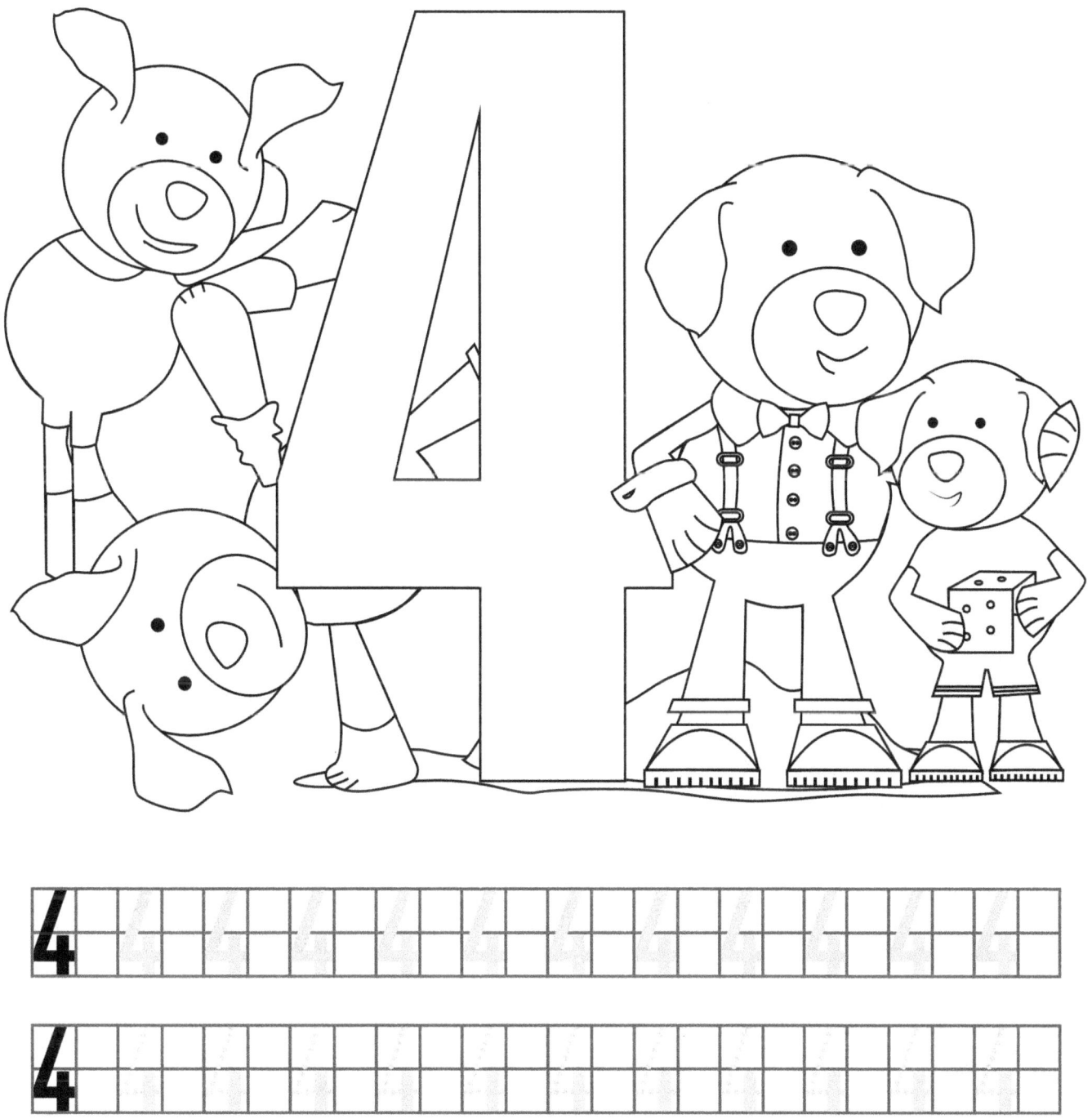

FIVE

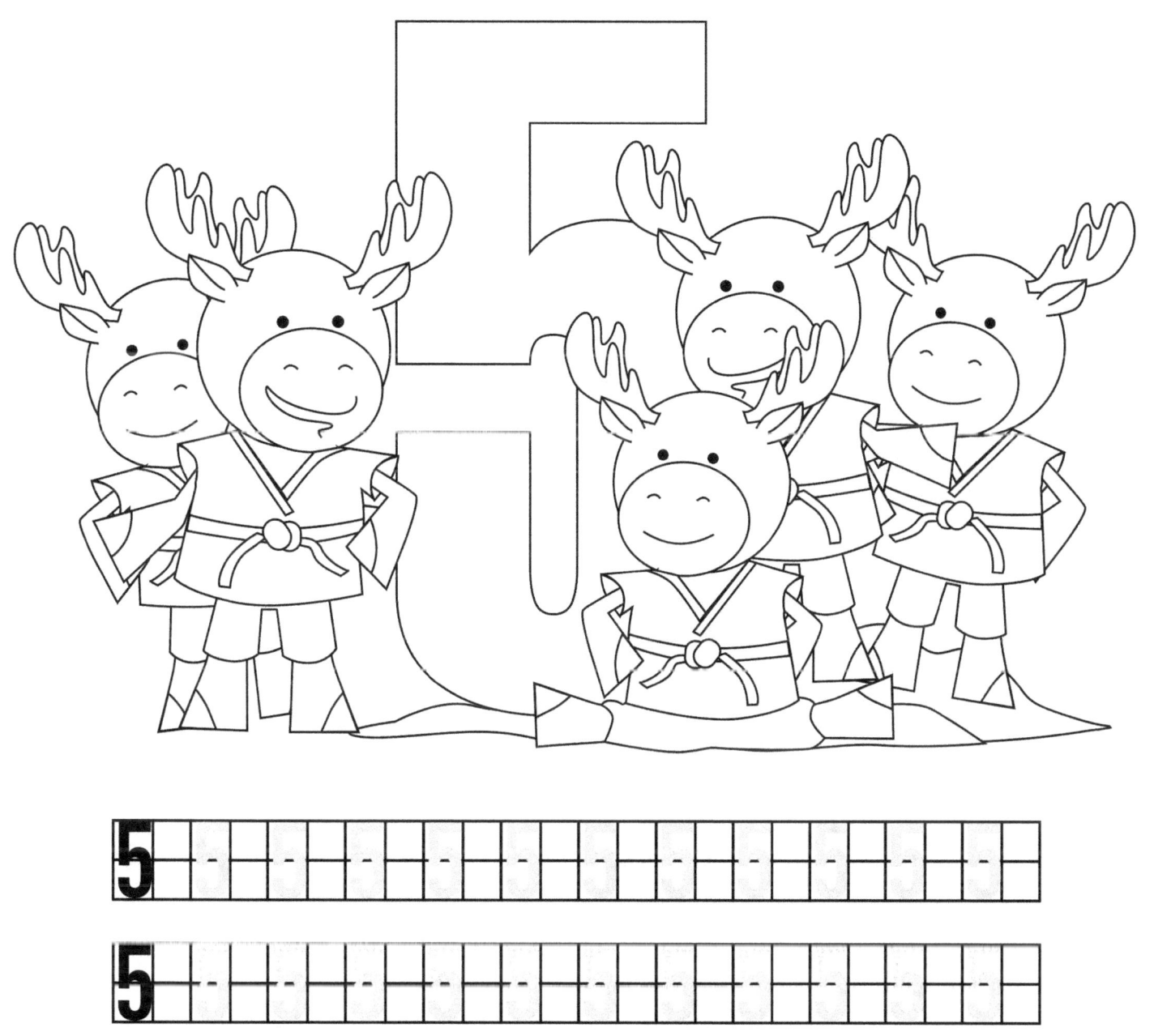

SIX

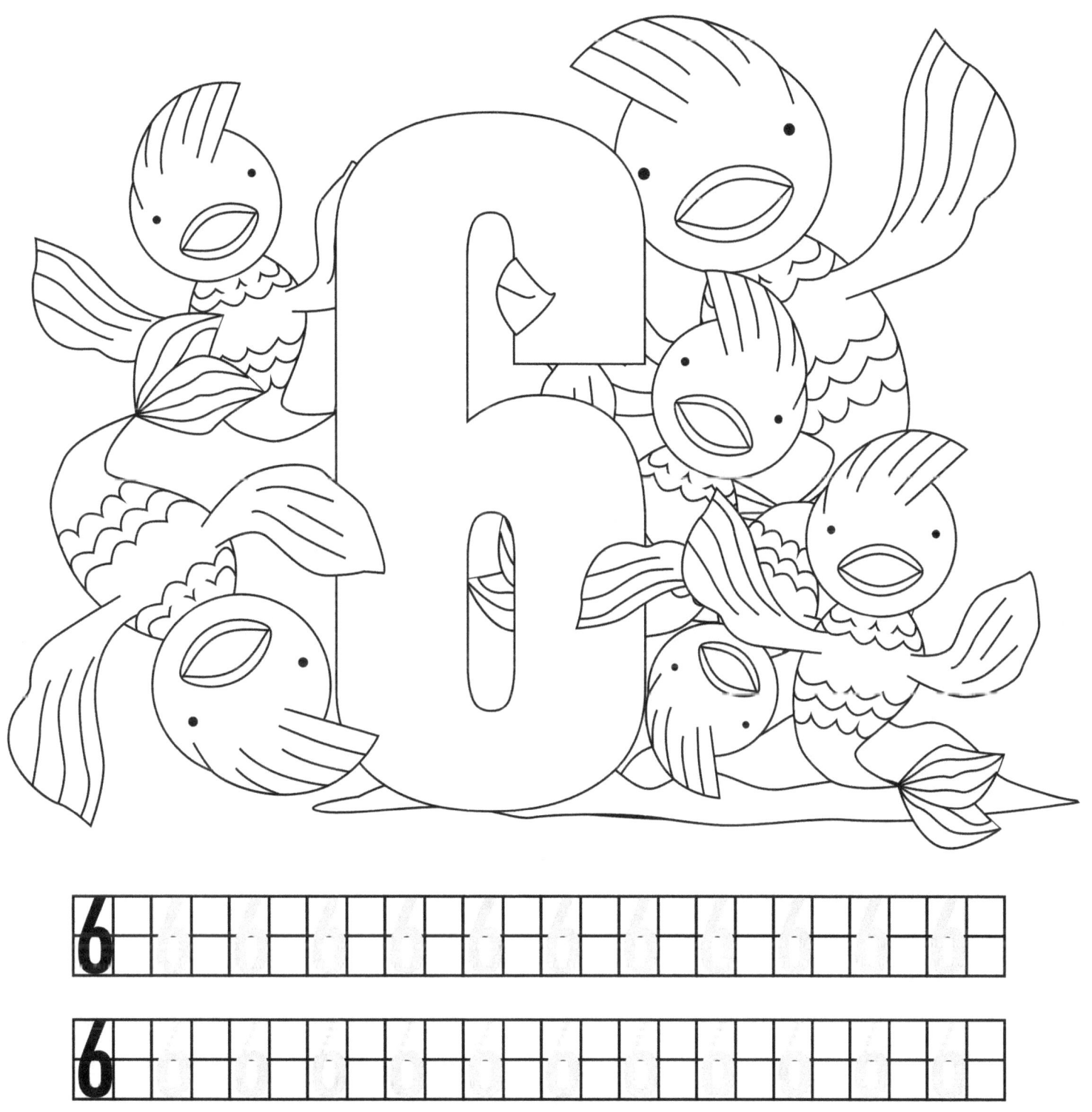

SEVEN

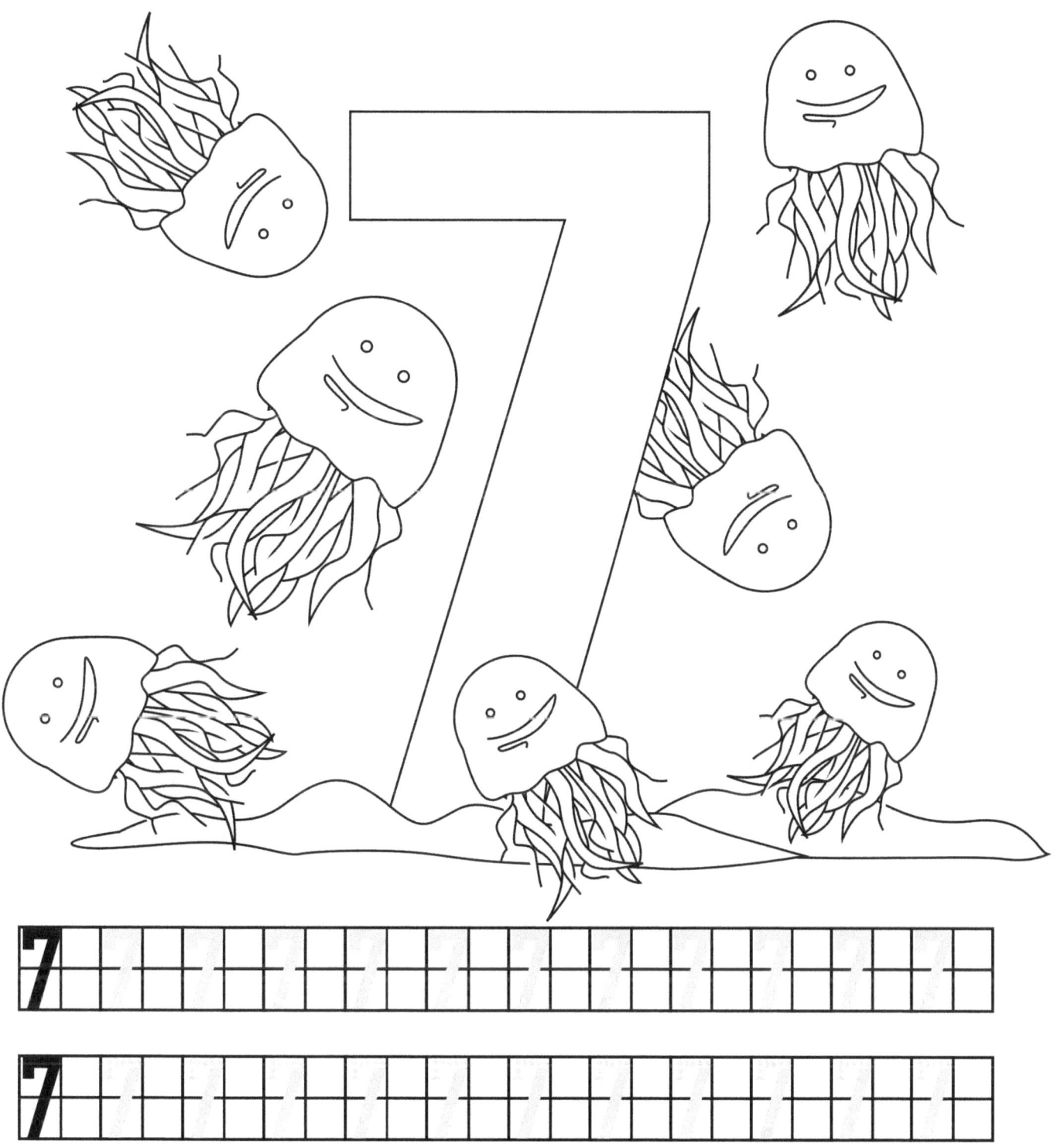

EIGHT

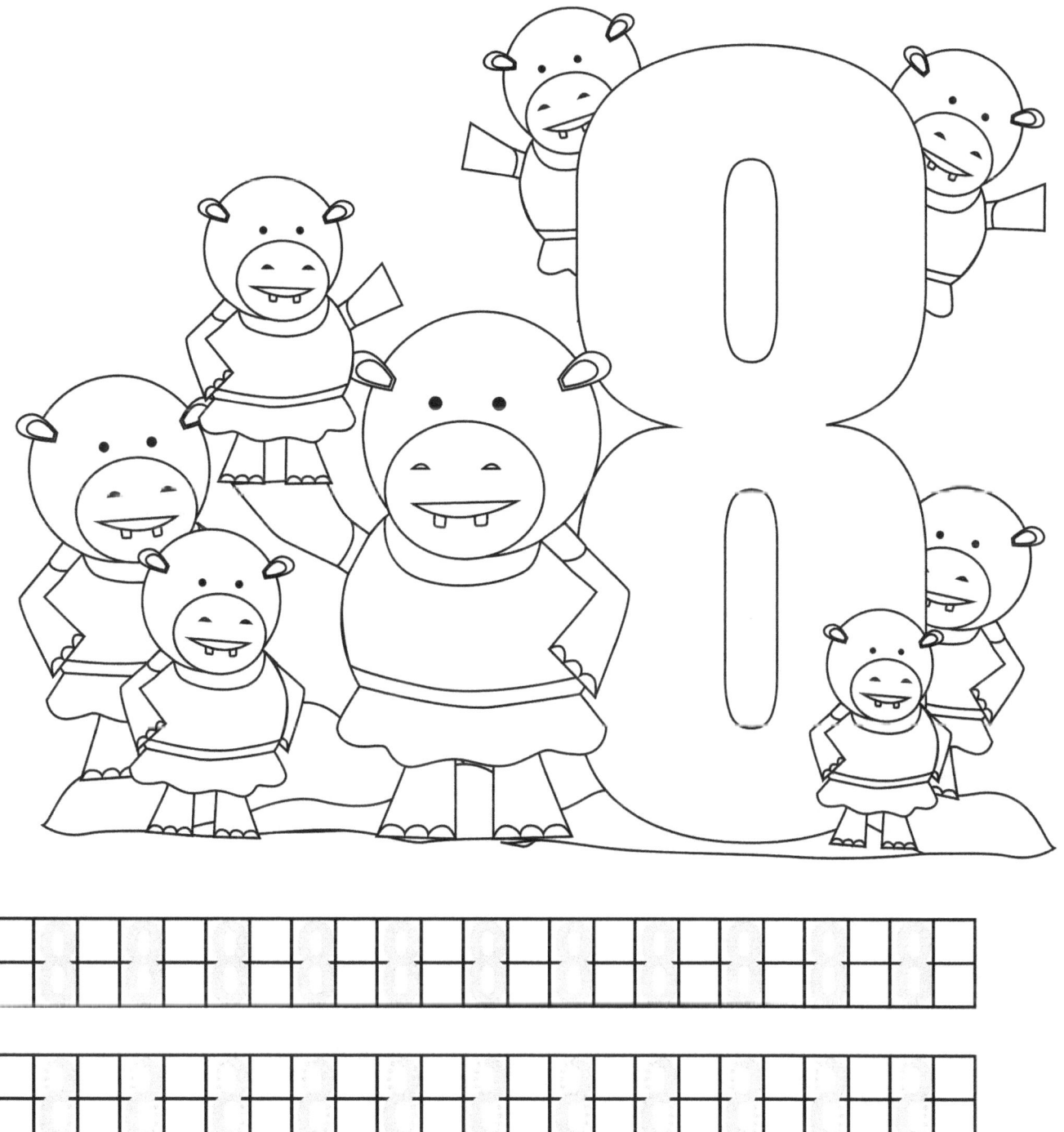

NINE

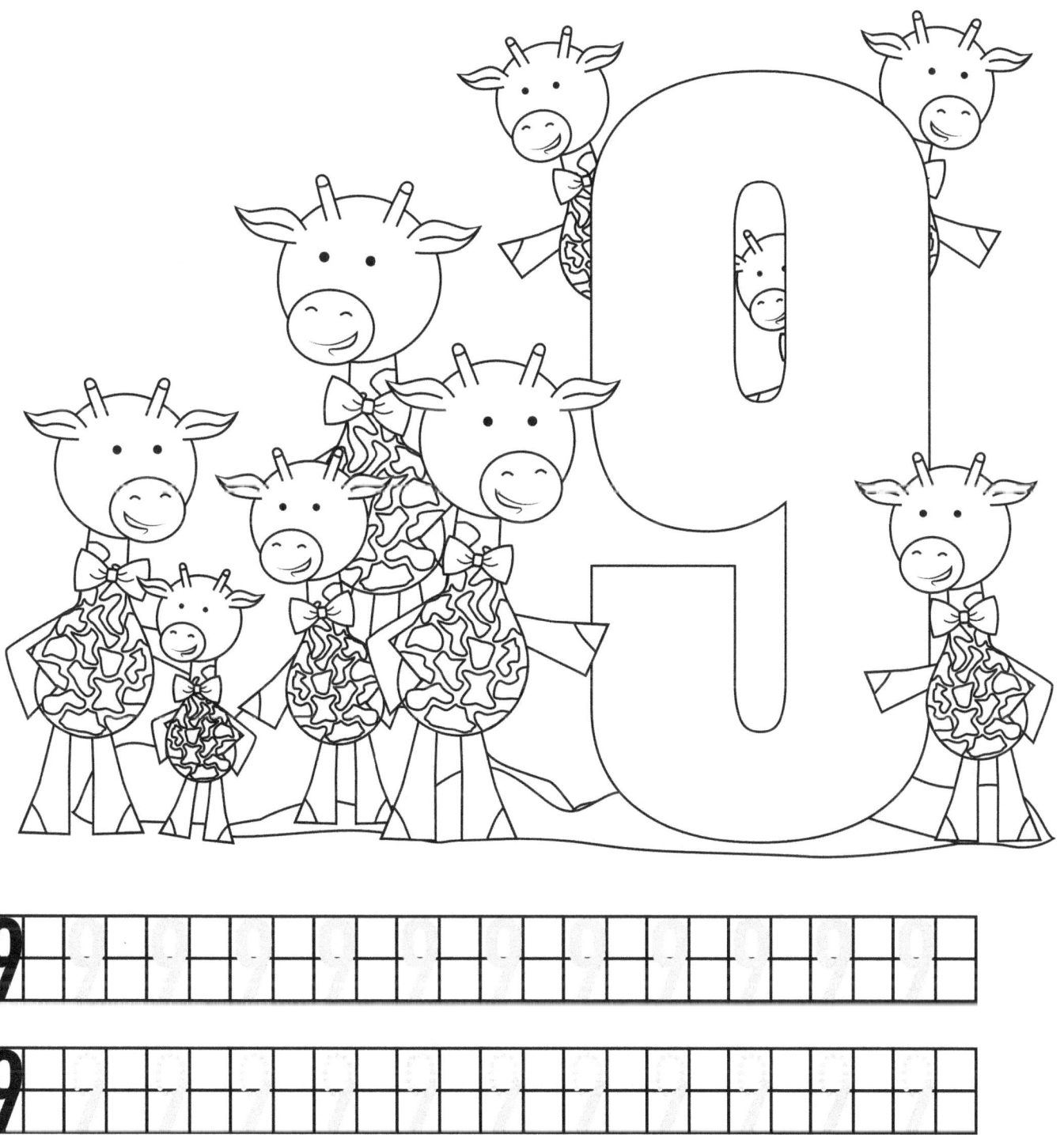

9
9

Find the way

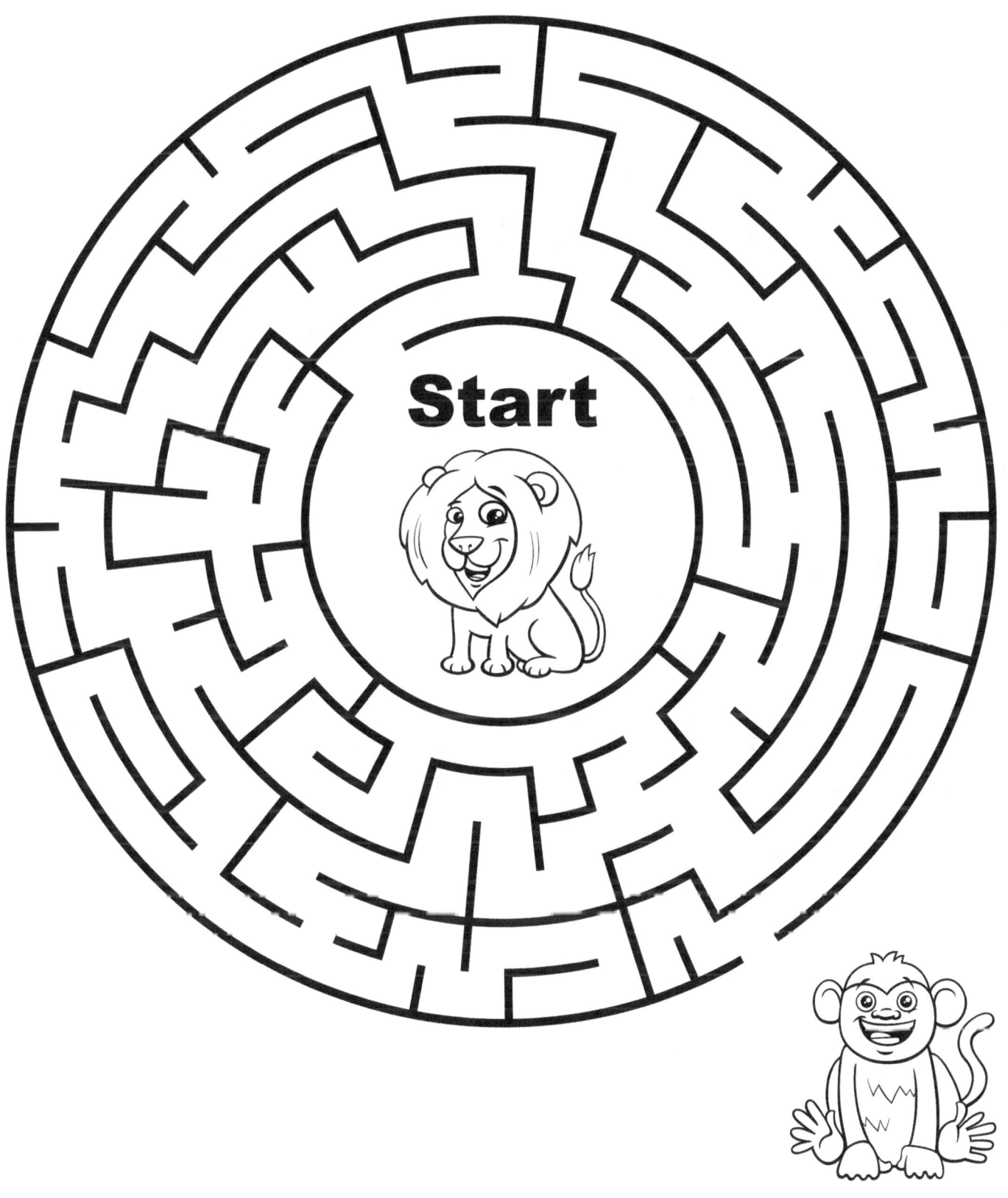

Start

Find the way

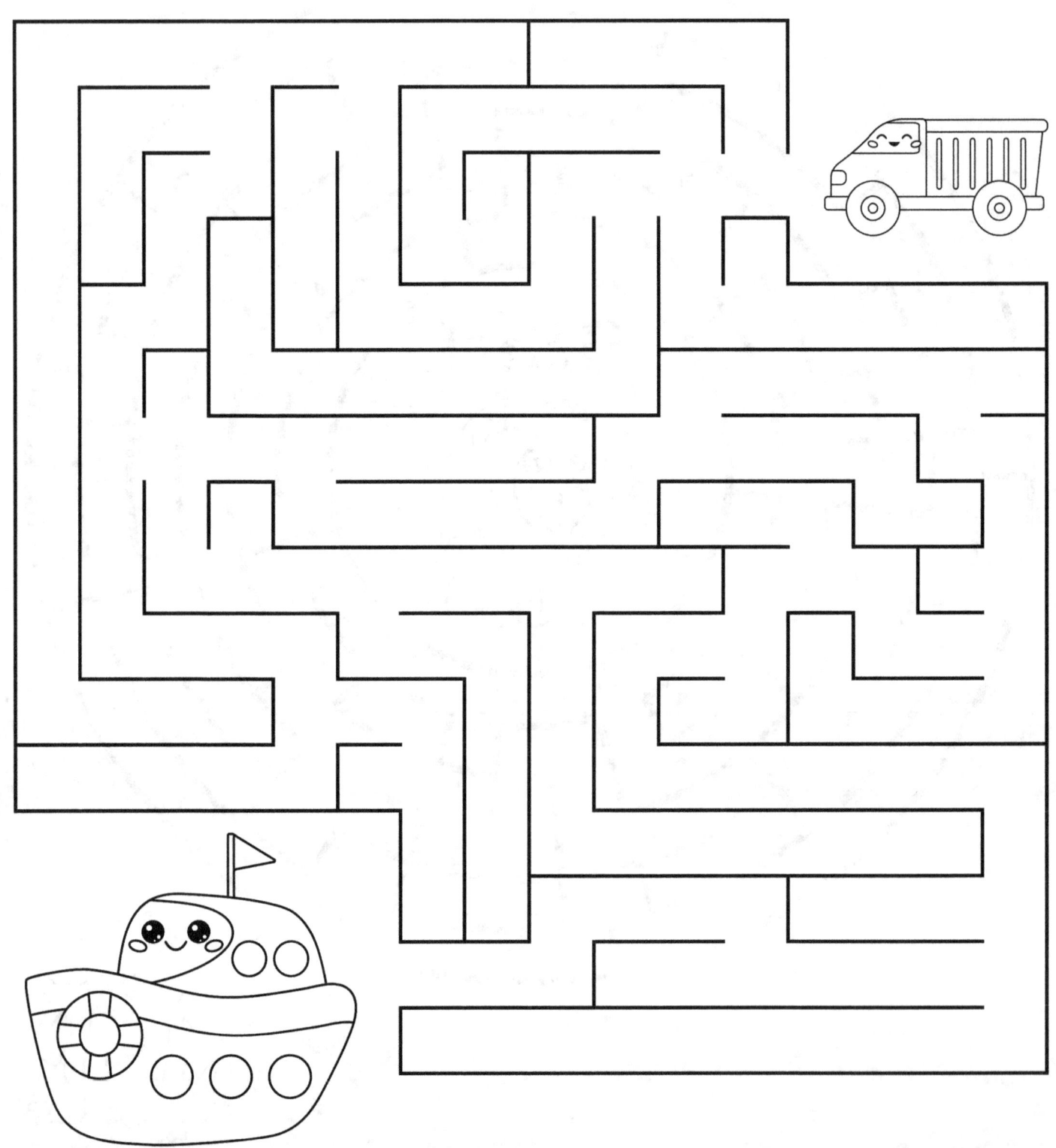

Find the way

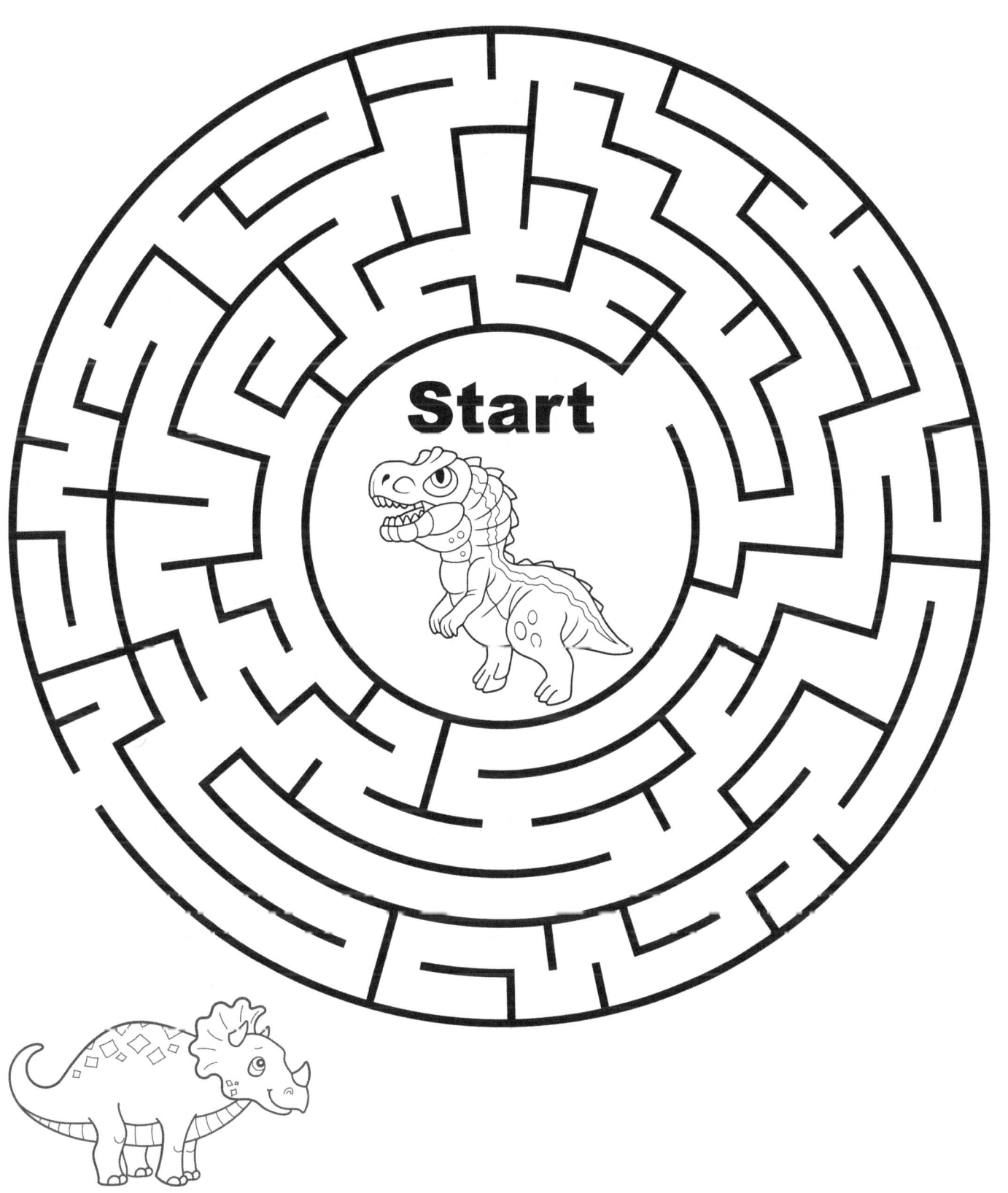

Start

Find the way

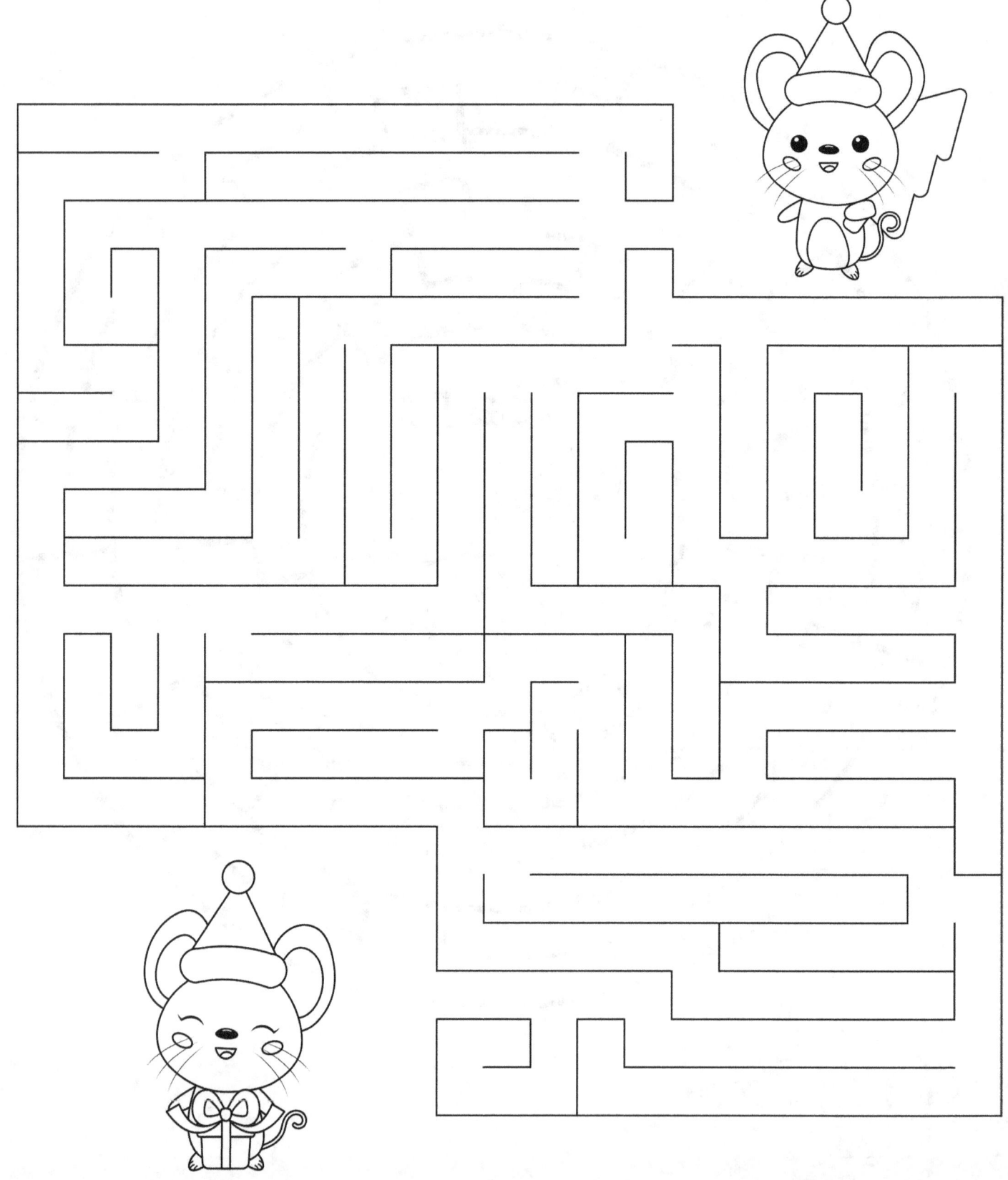

Find the way

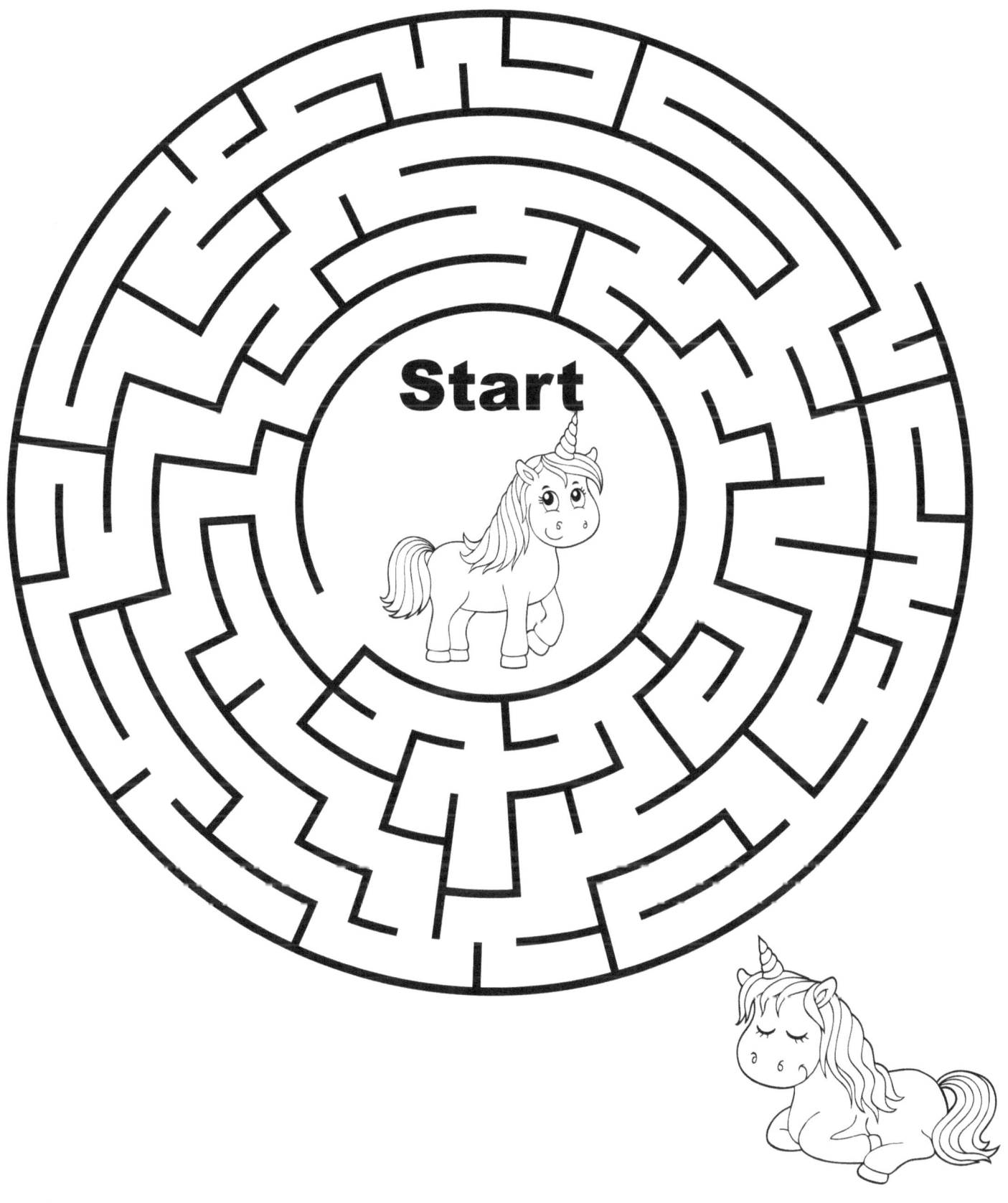

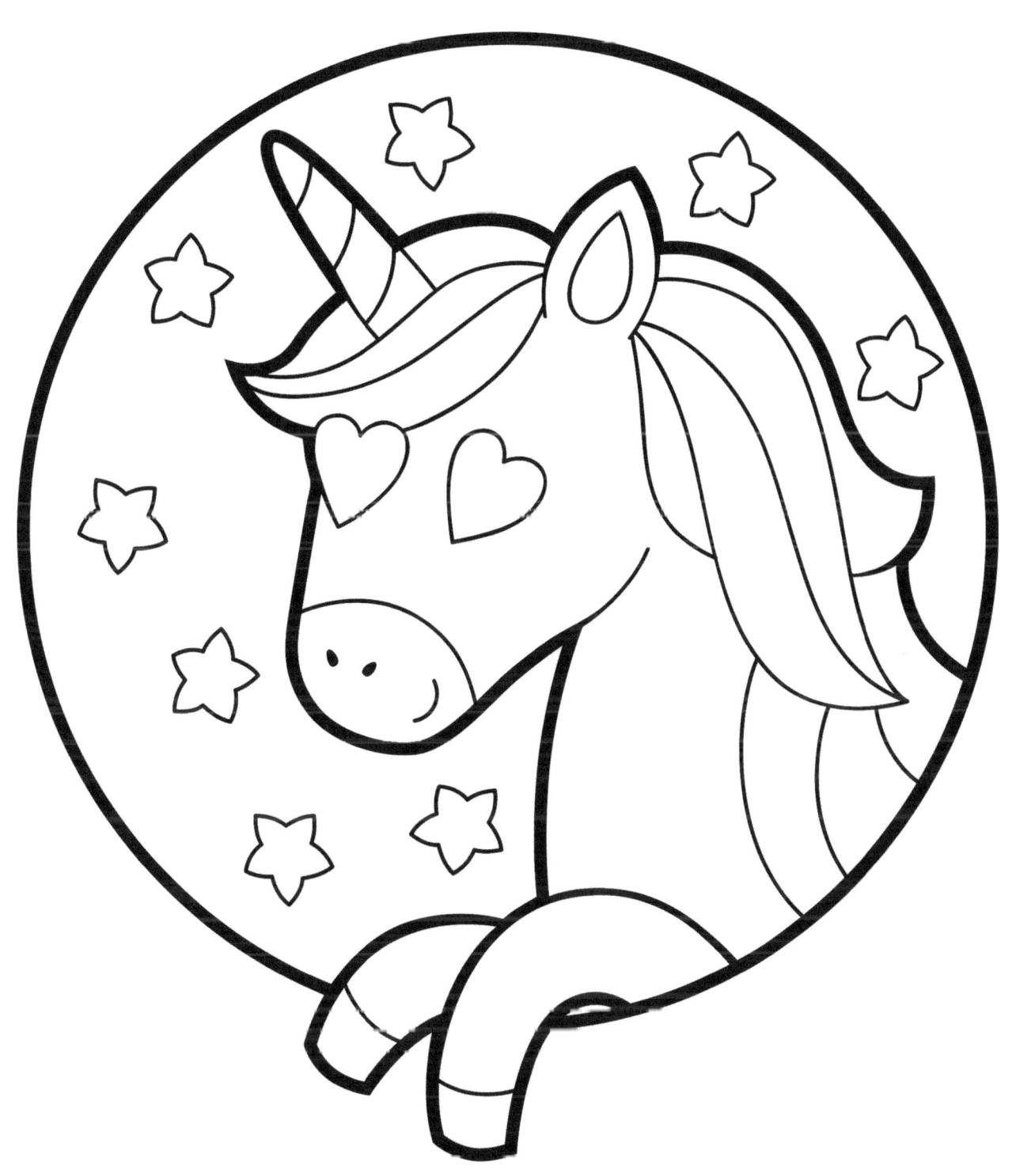

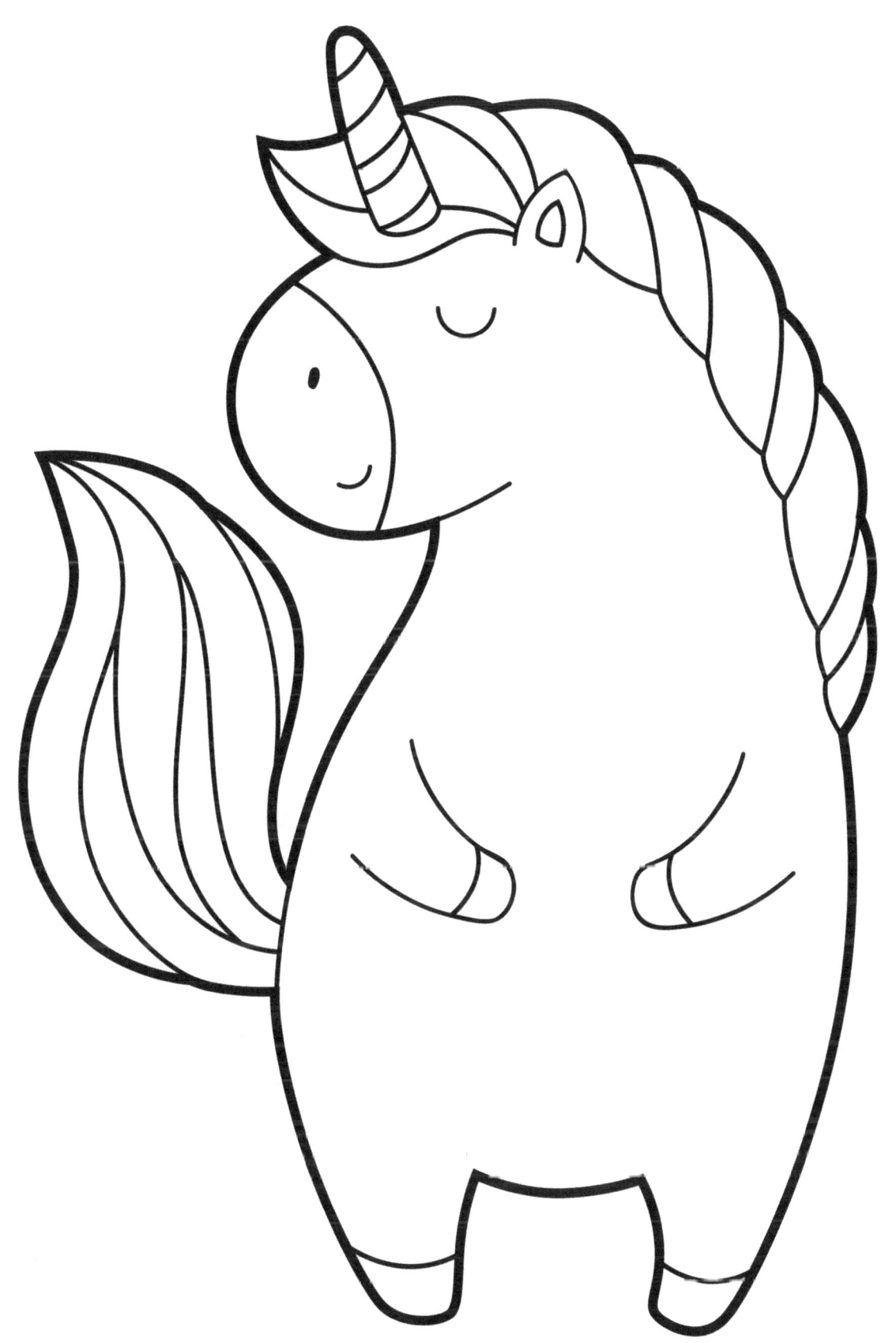

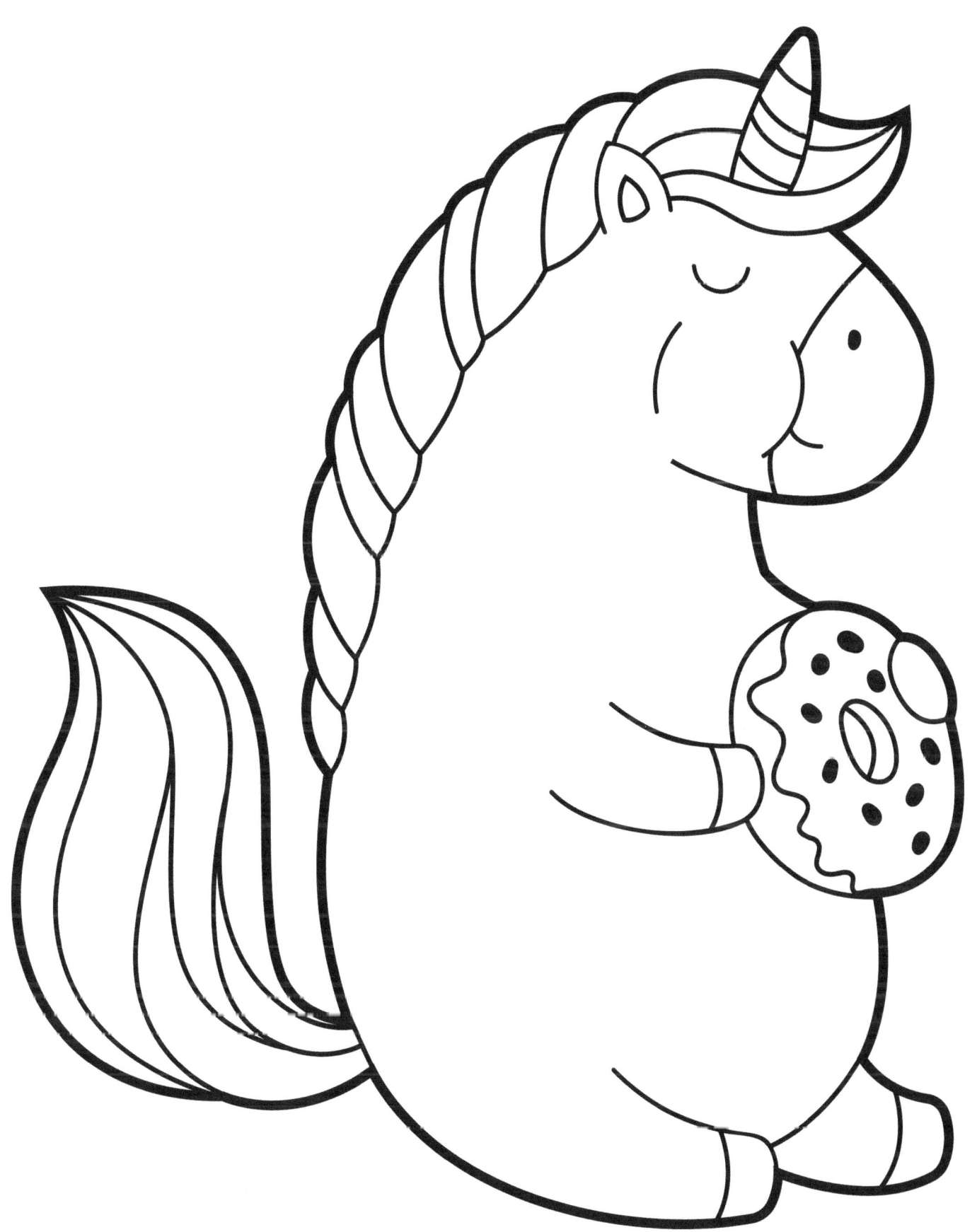

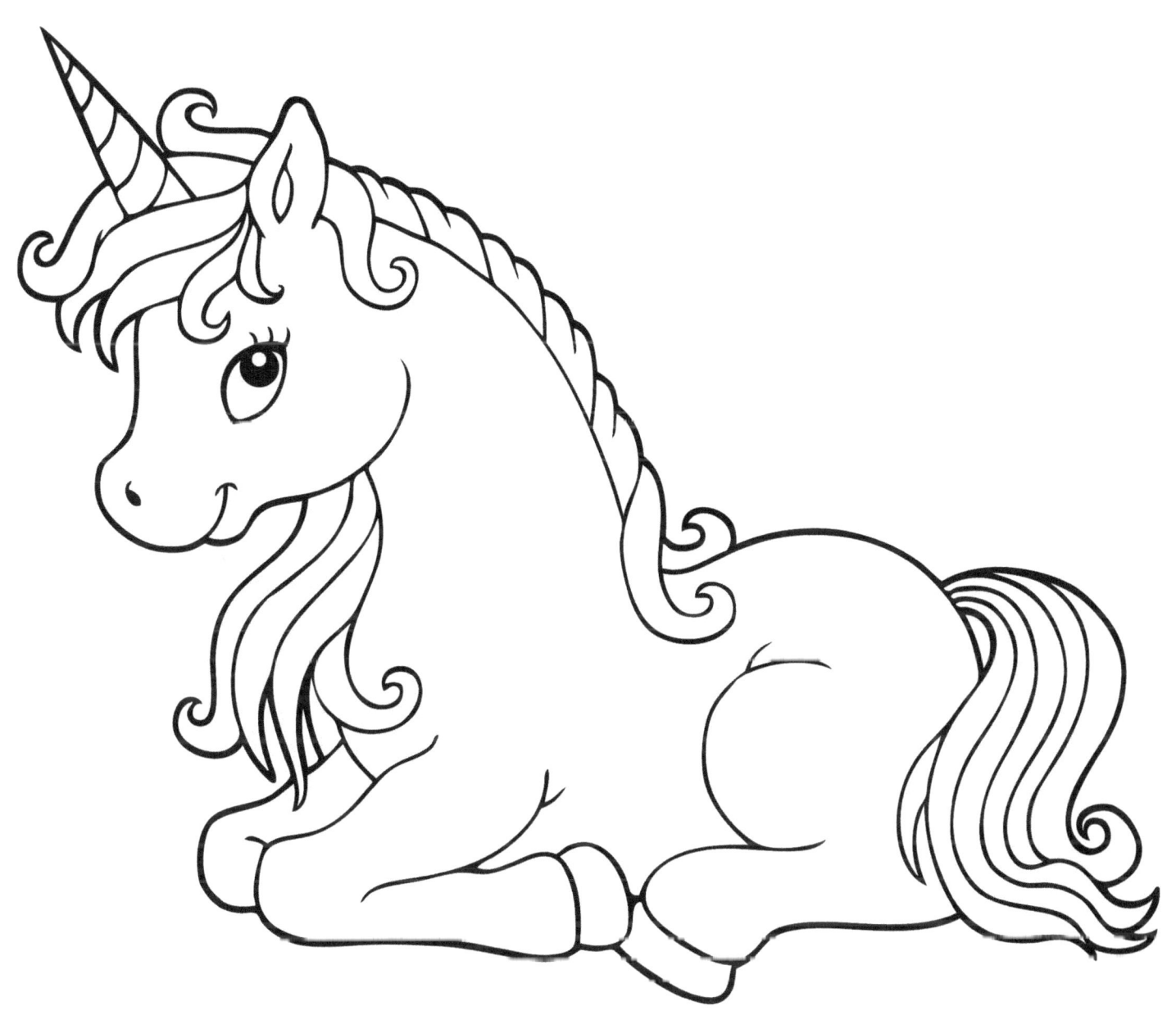

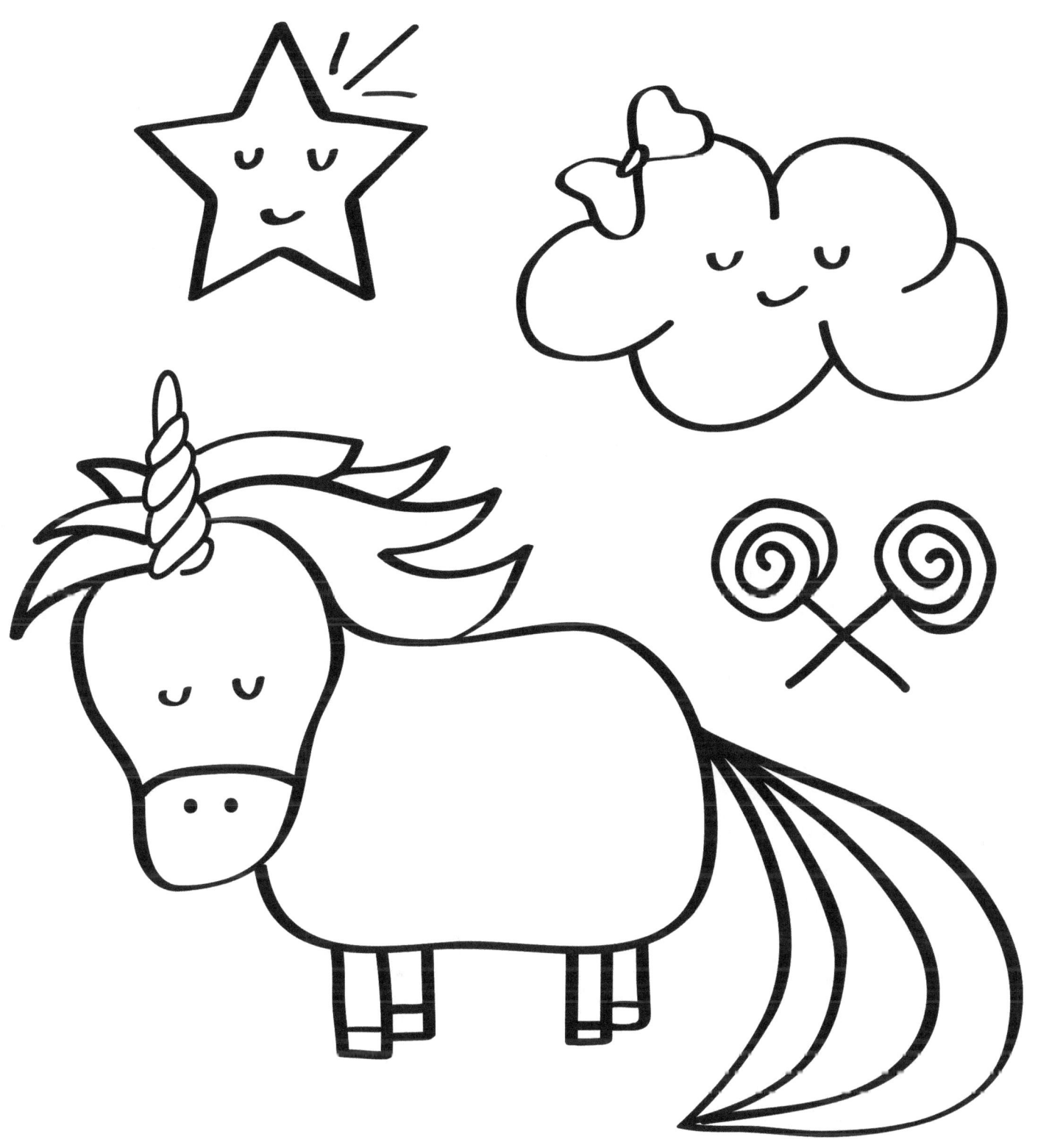

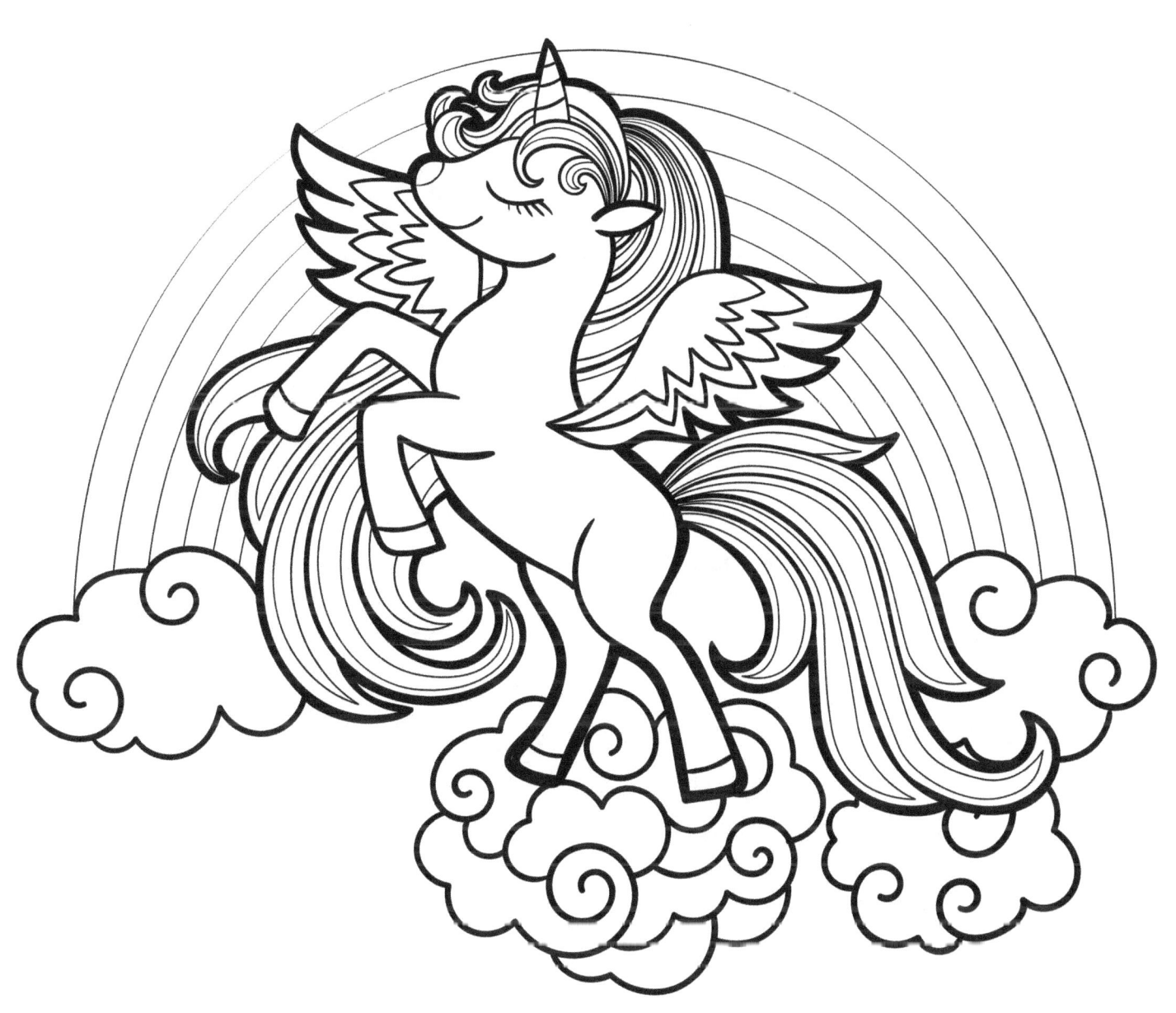

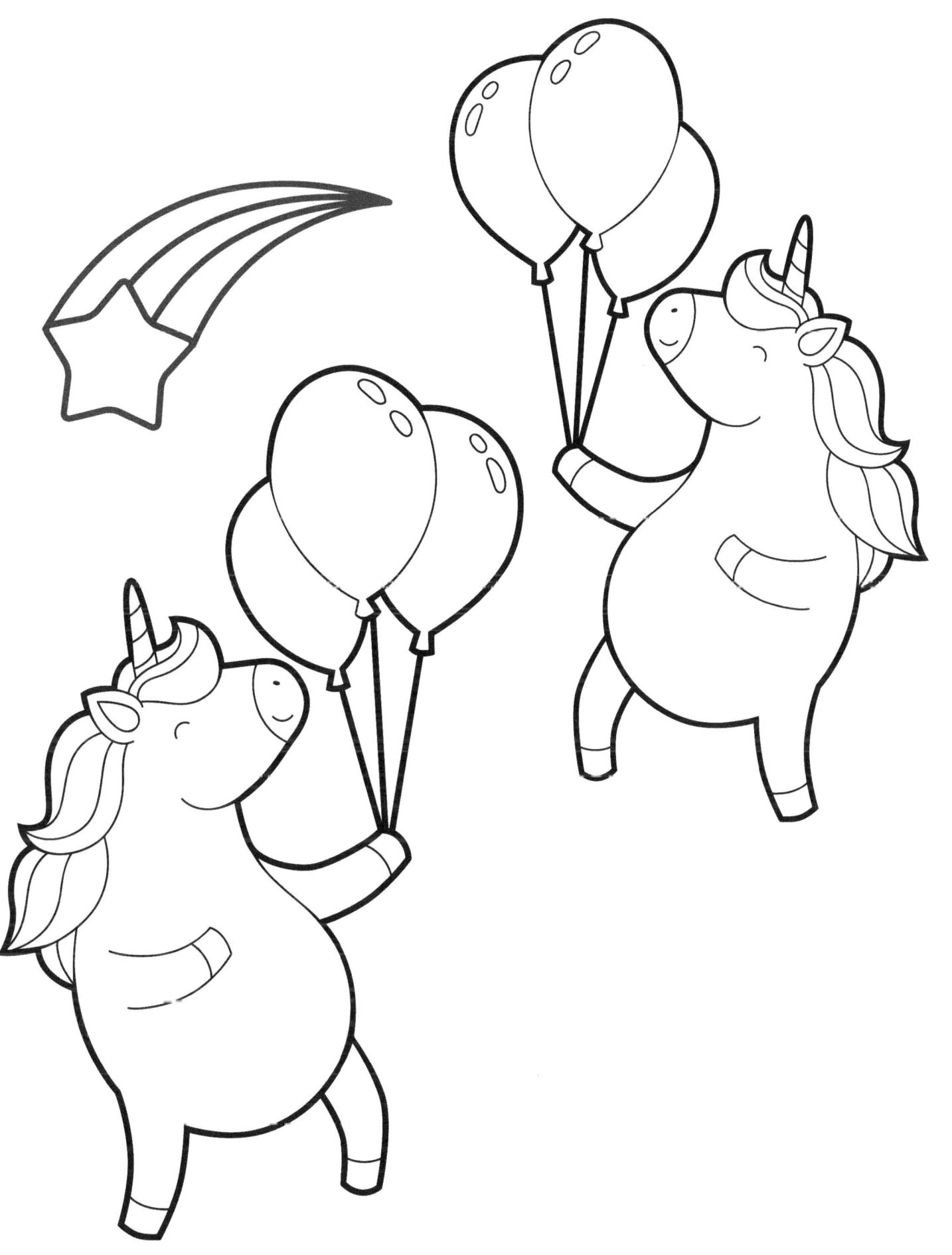

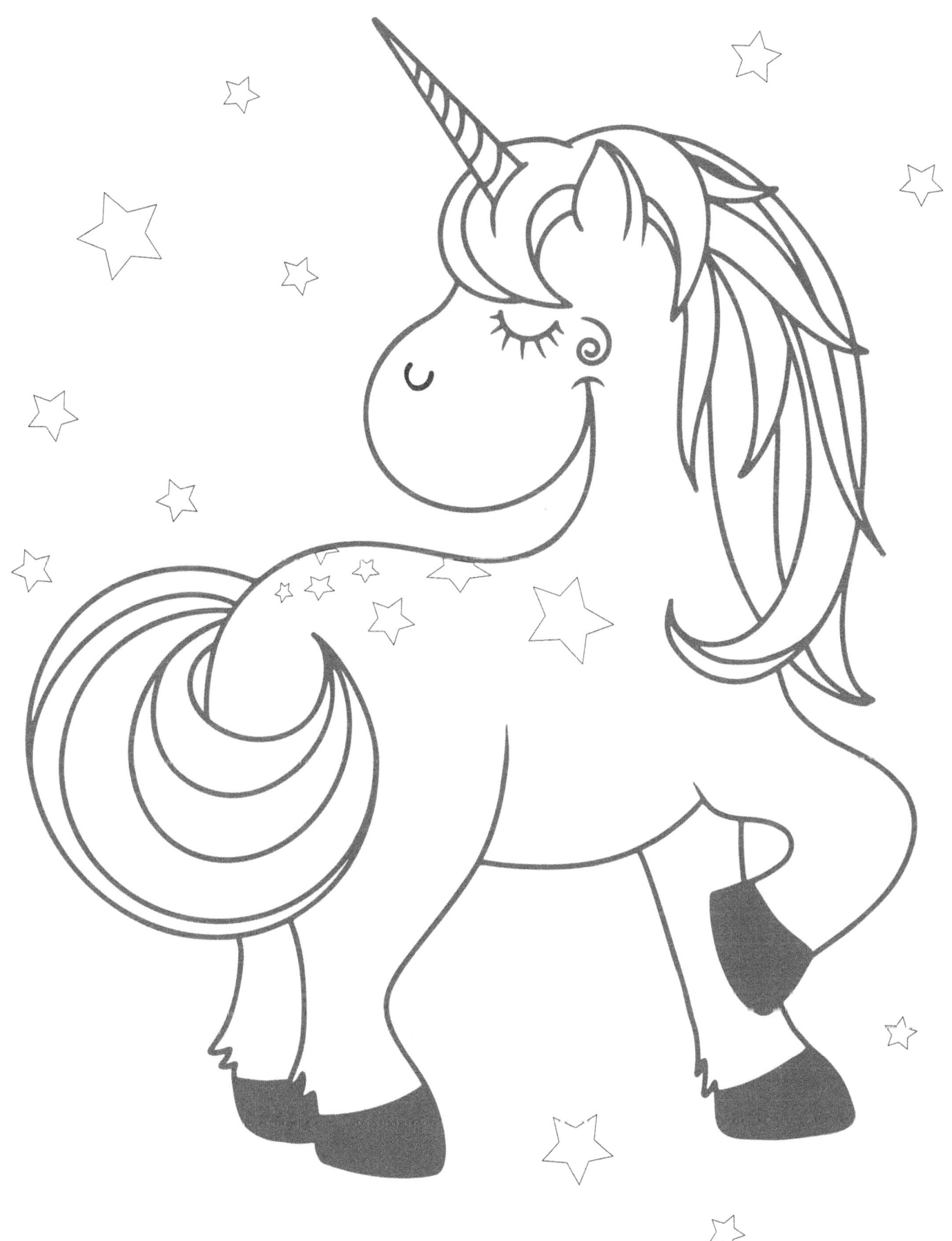

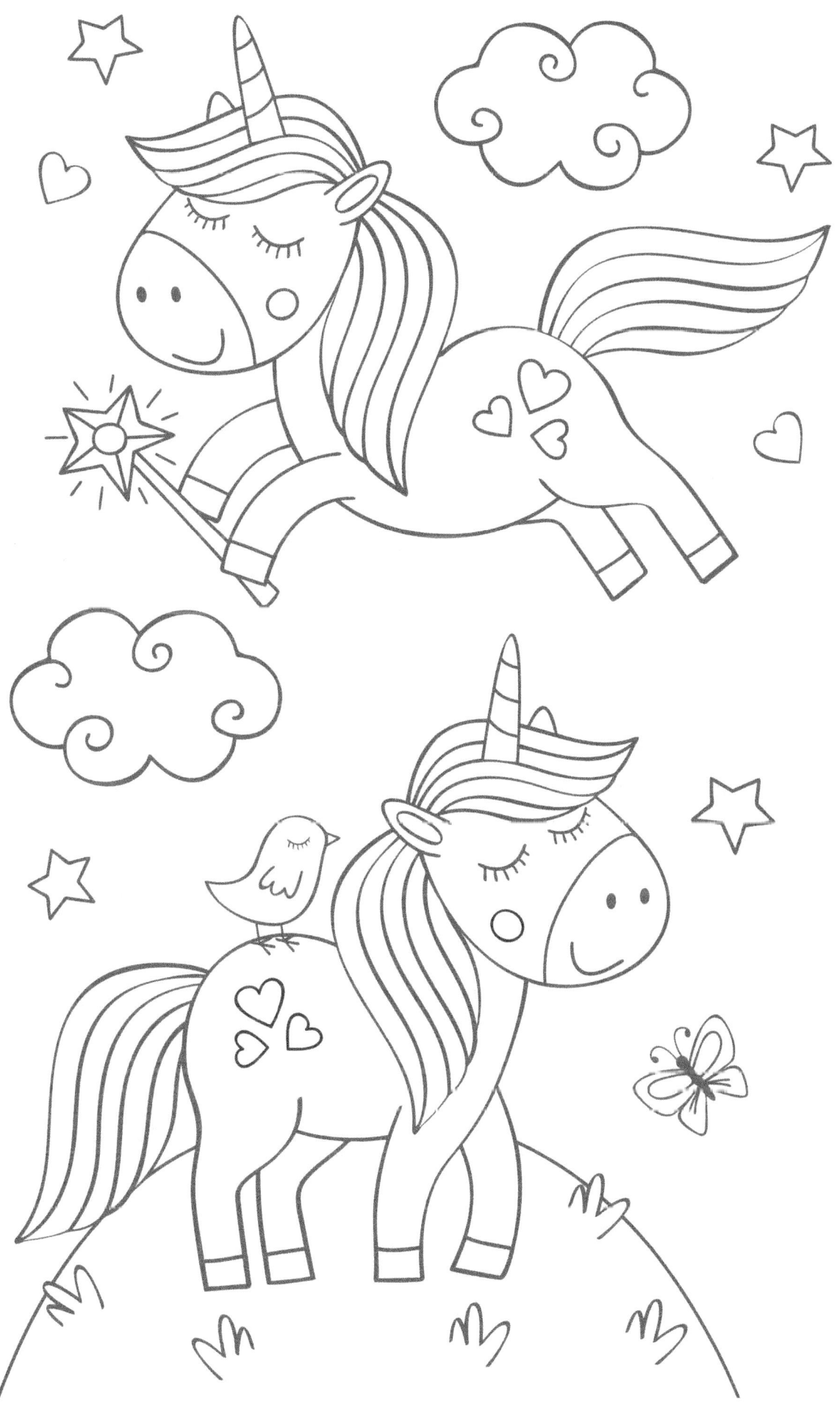

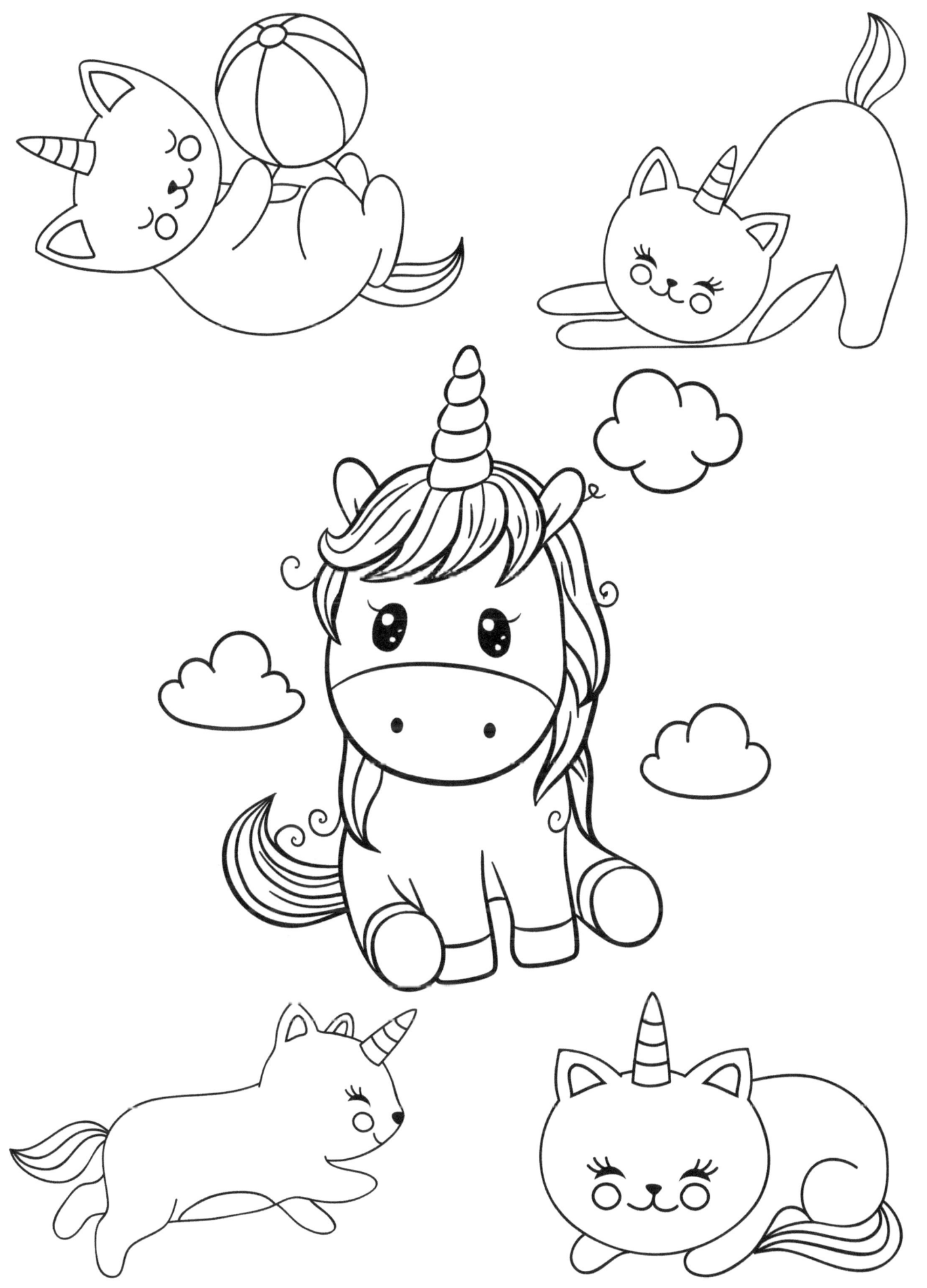

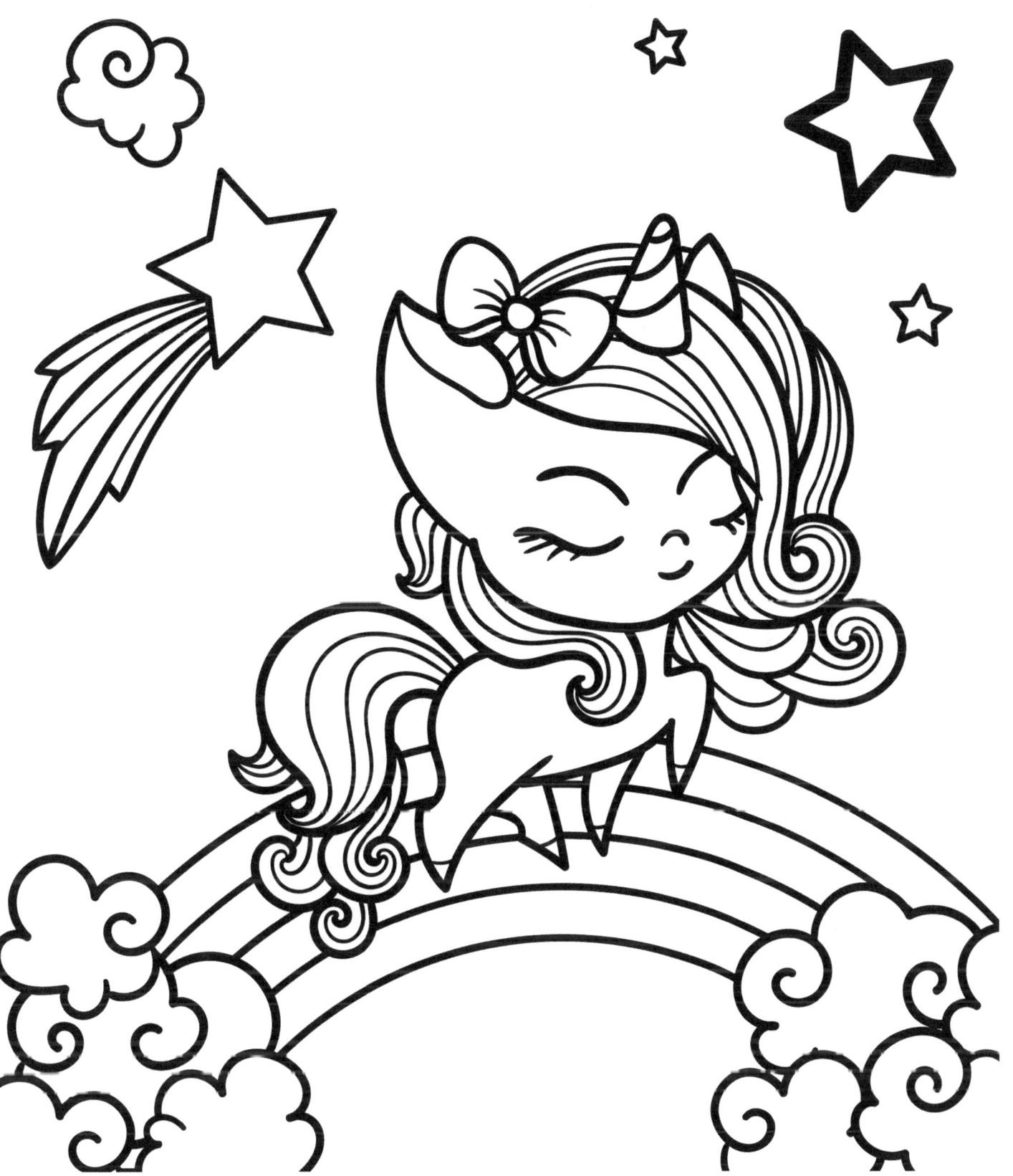

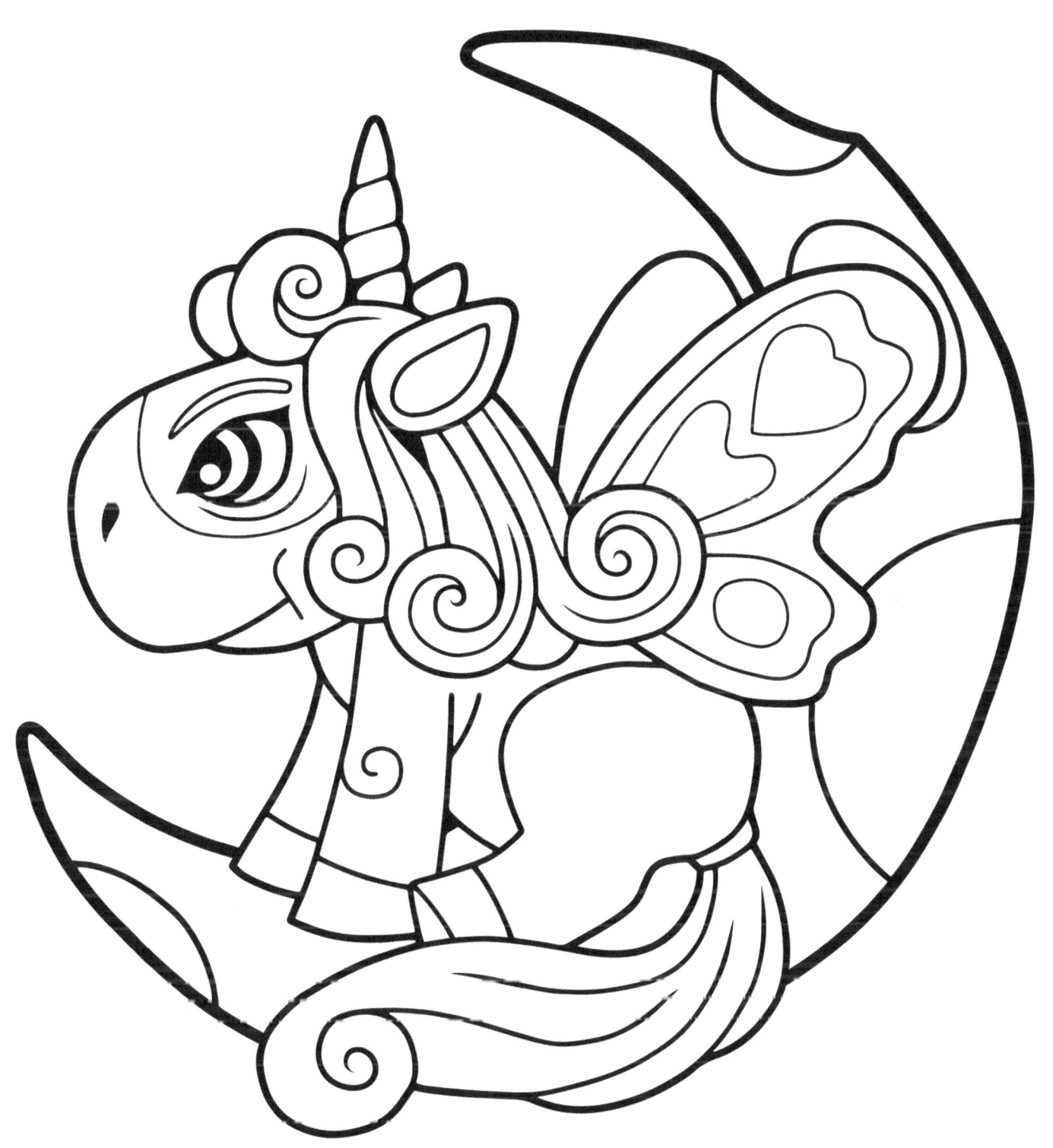

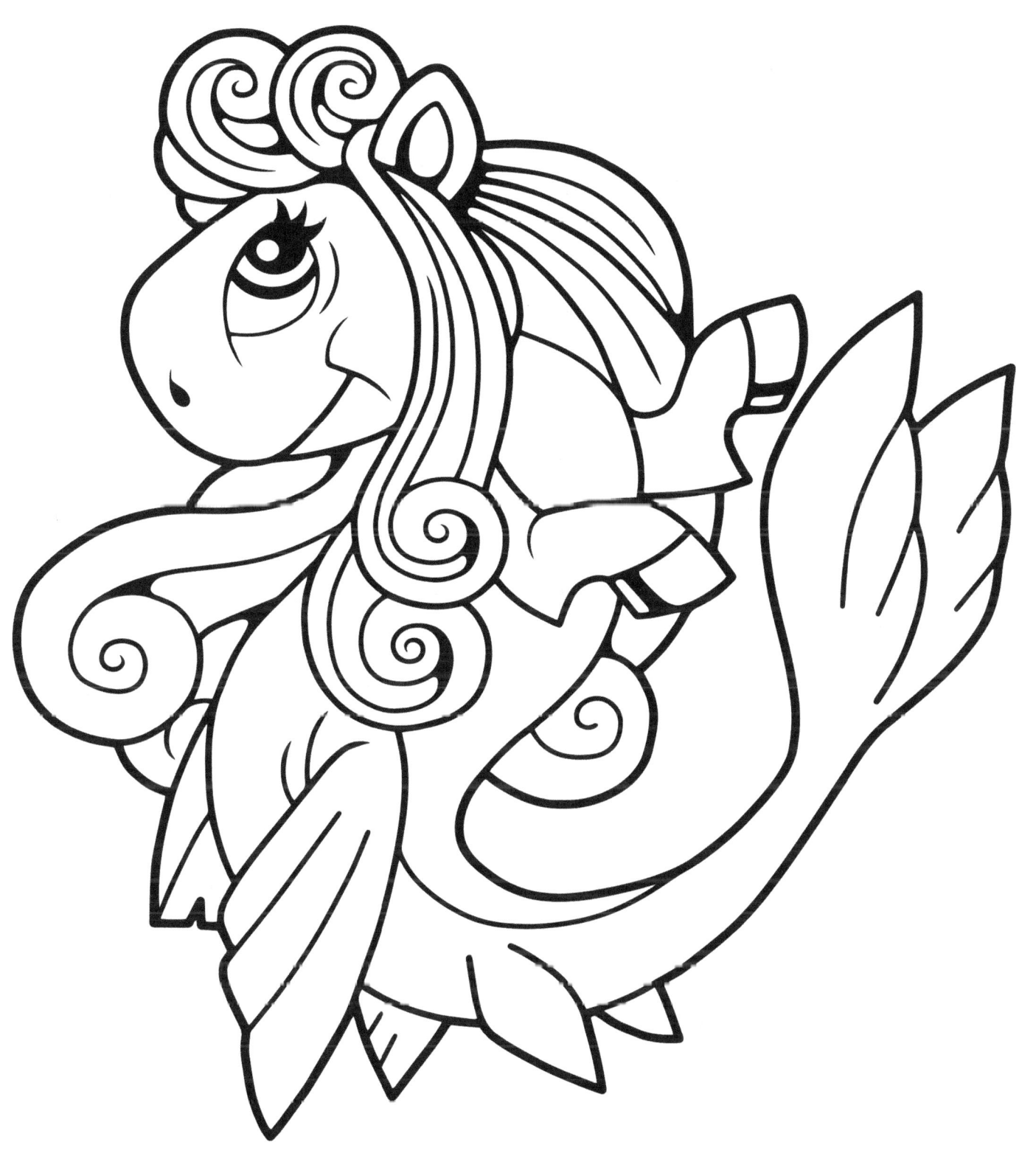

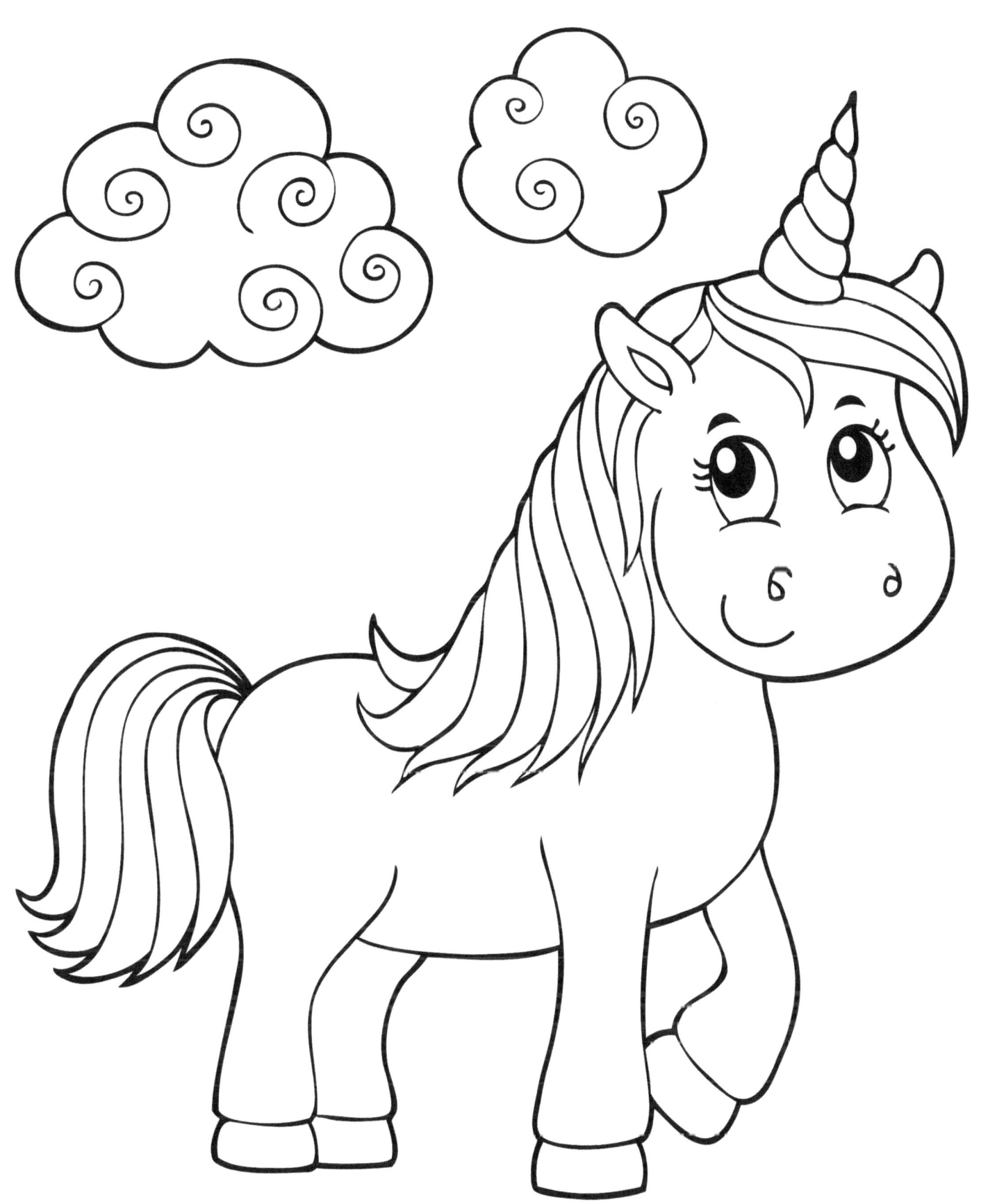

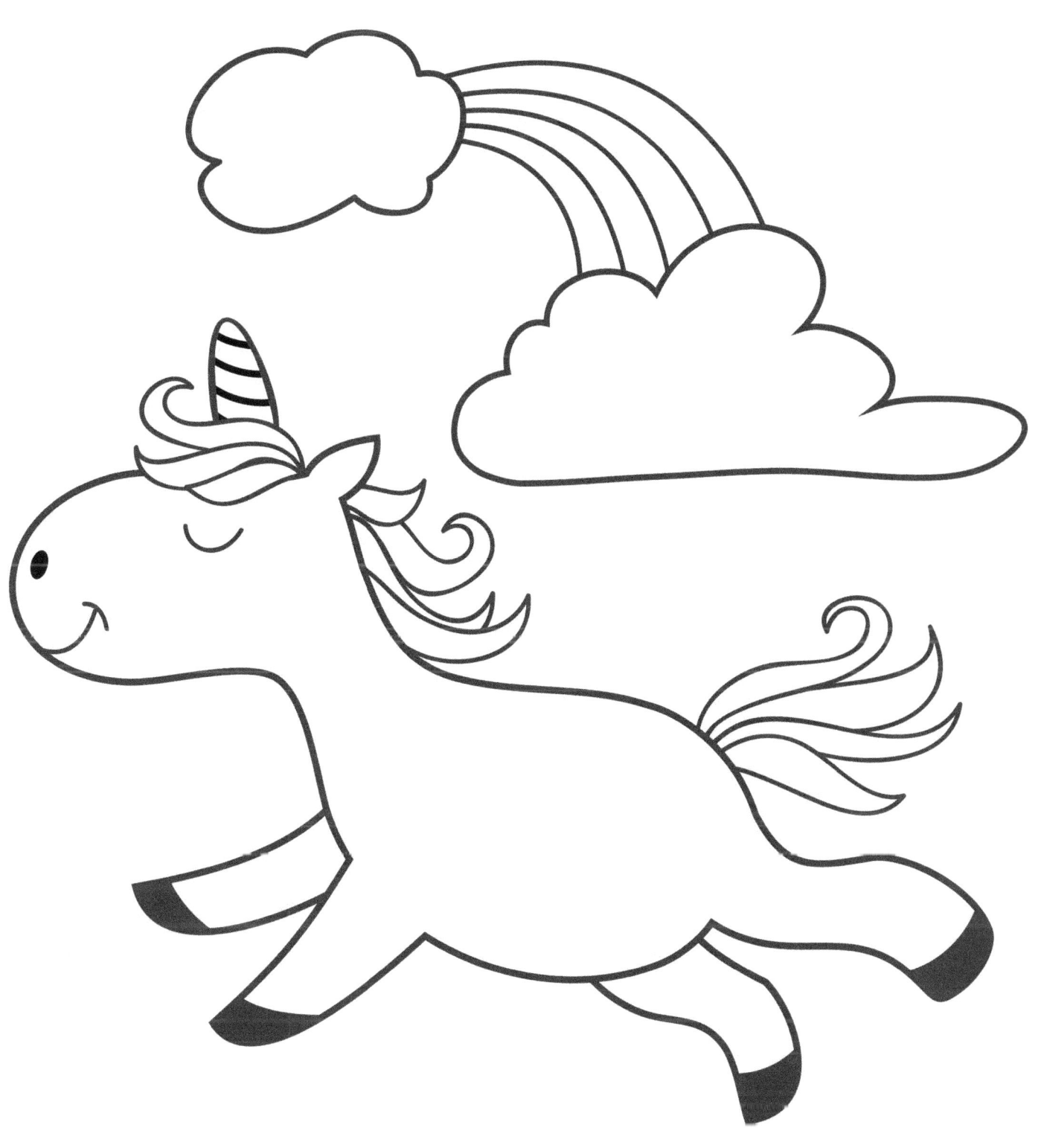

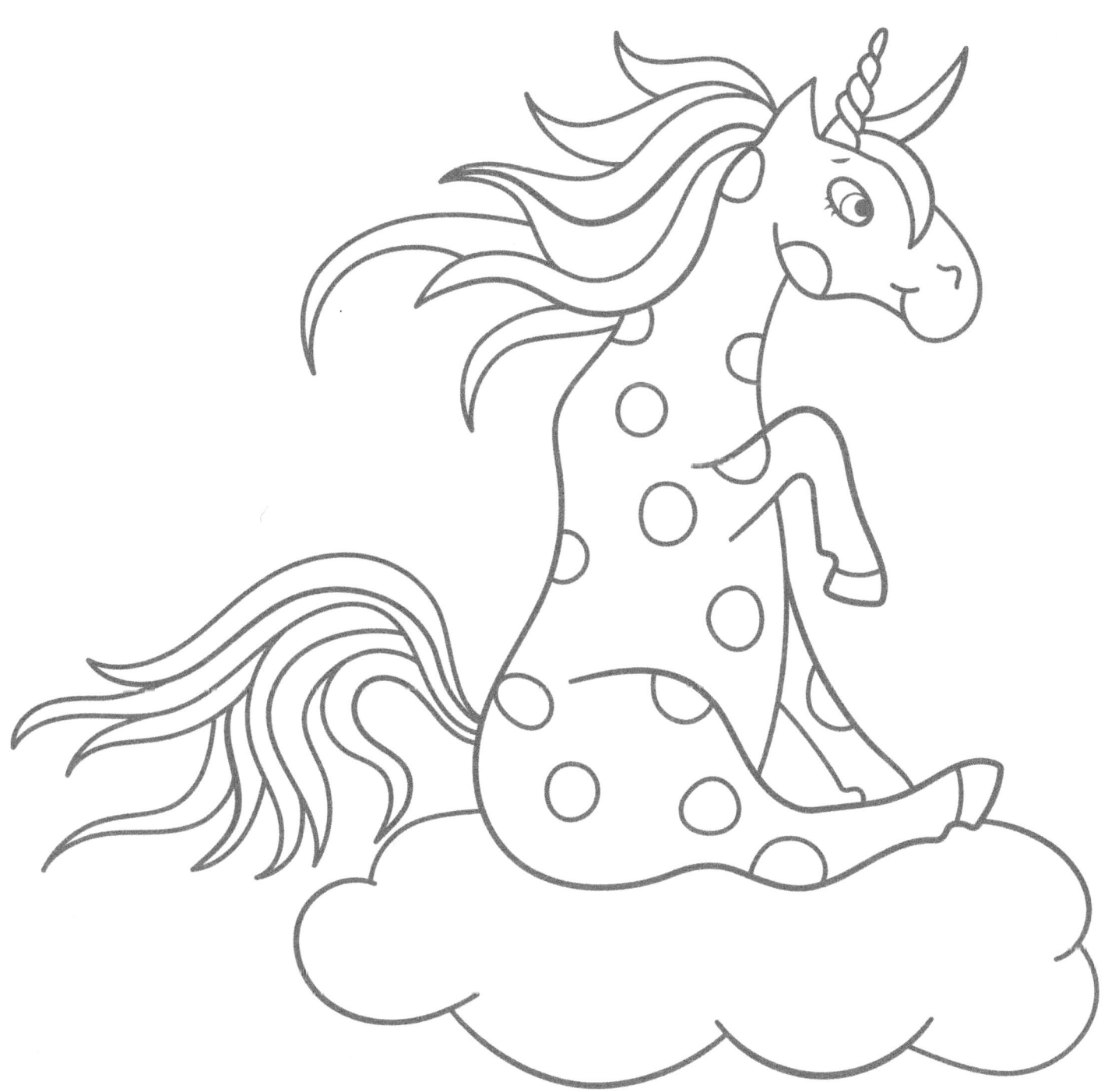

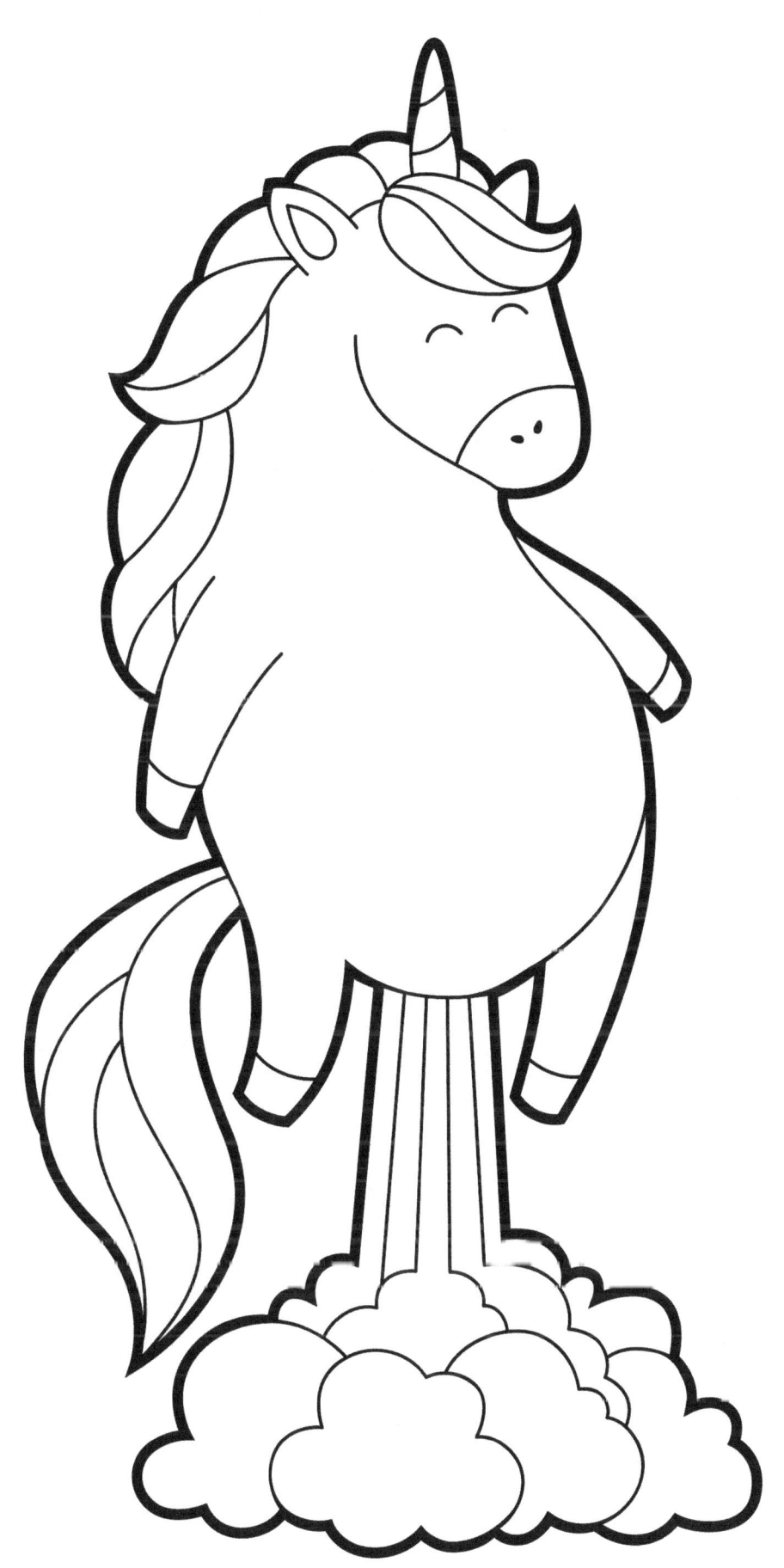

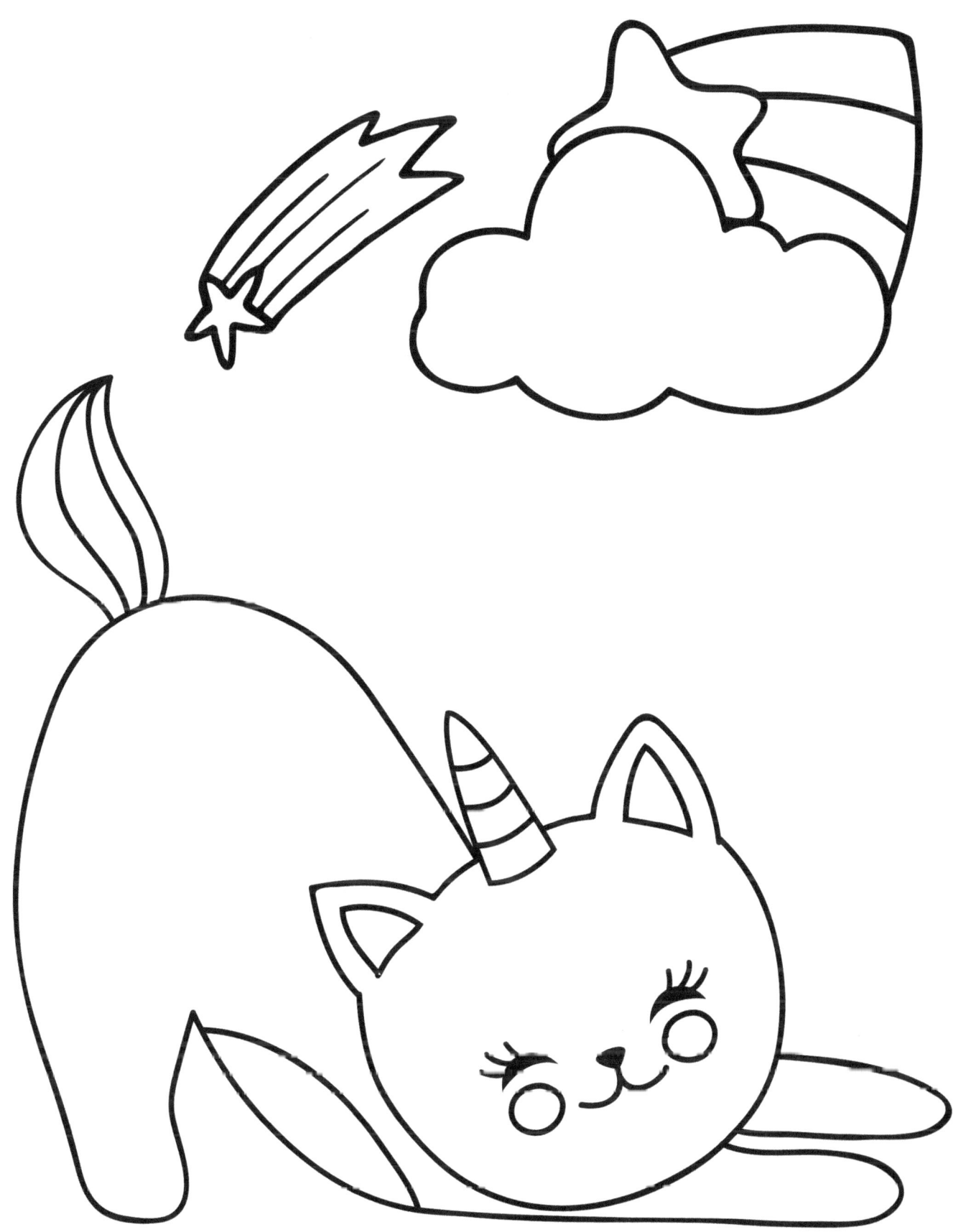

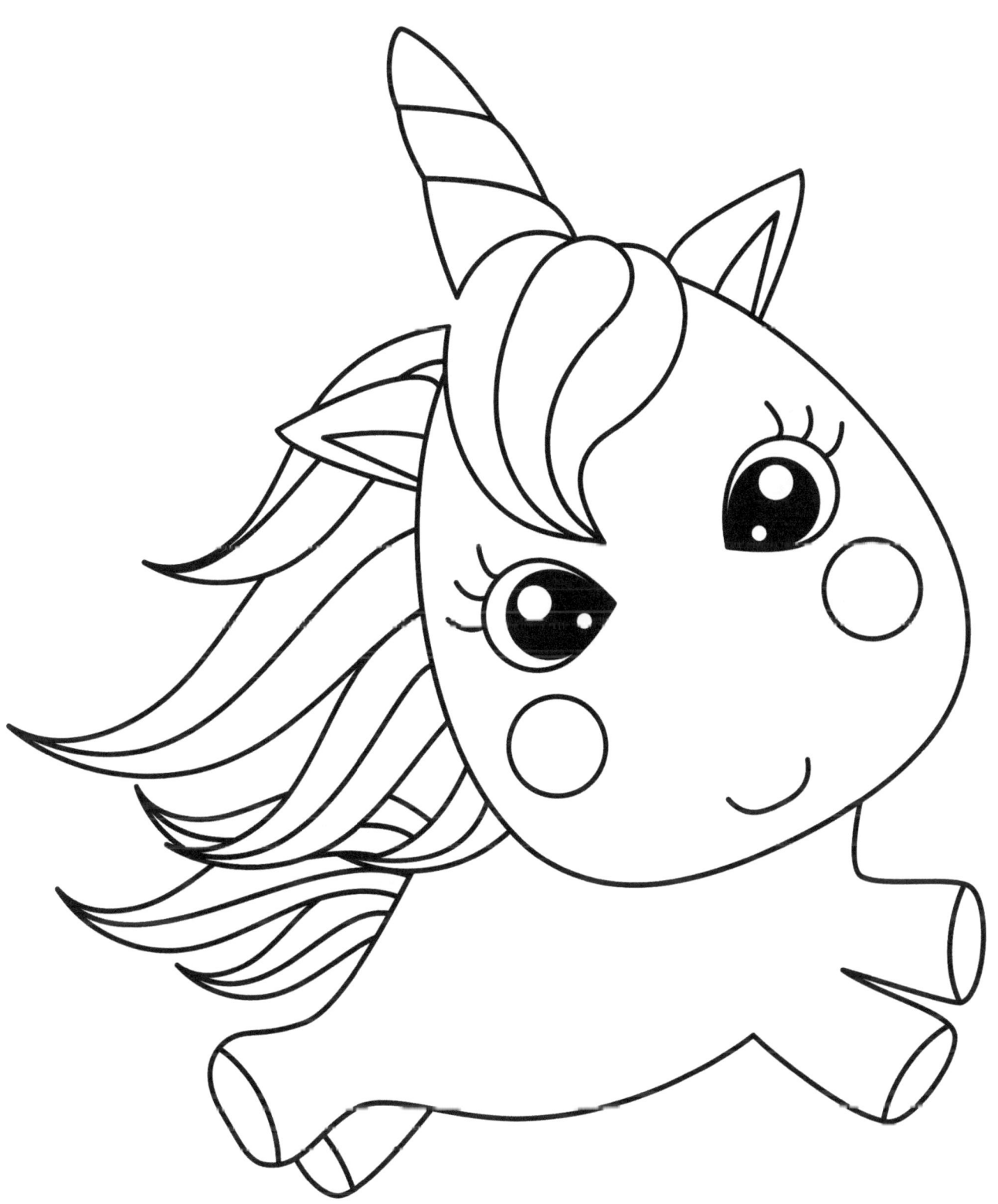

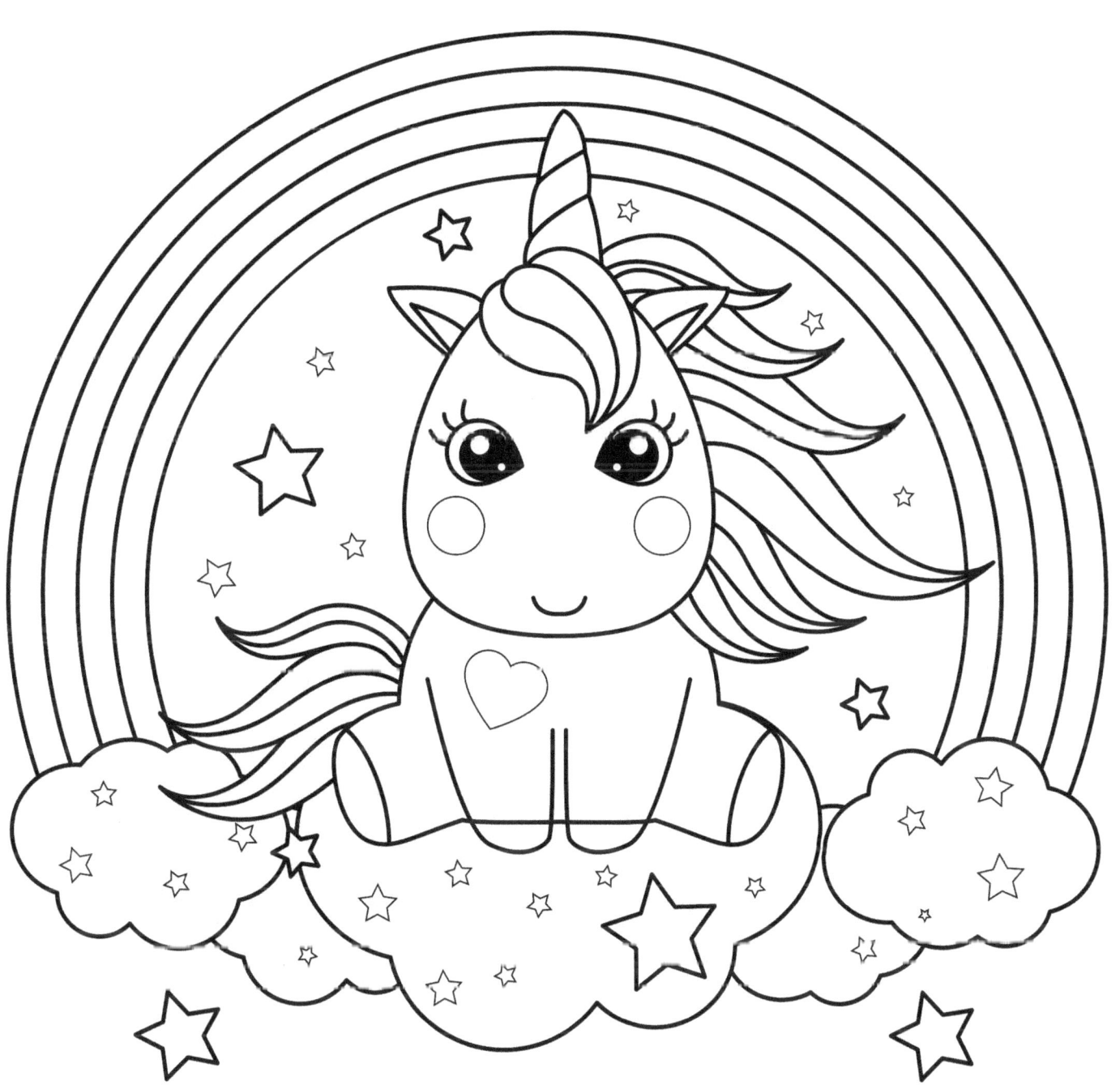

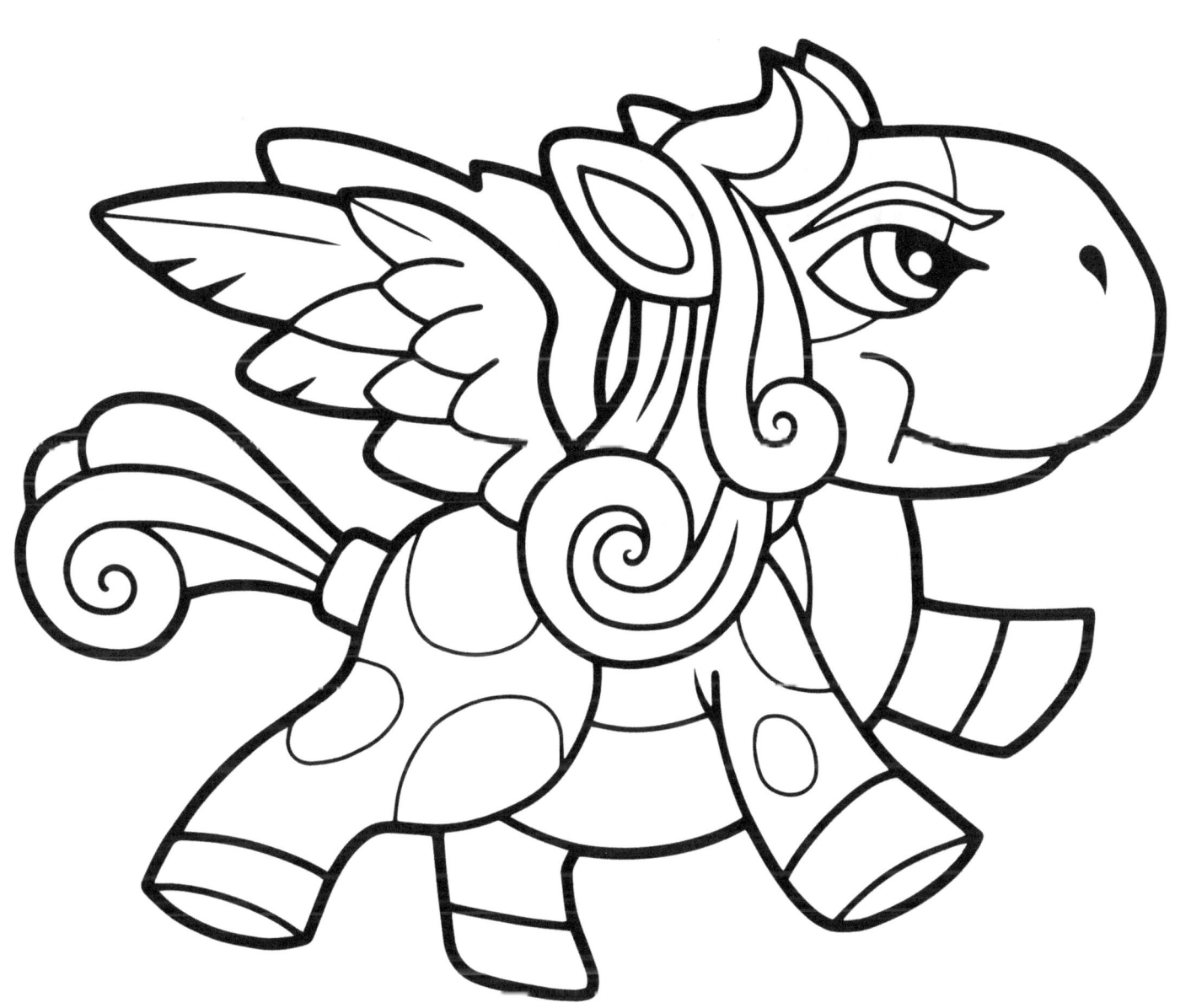

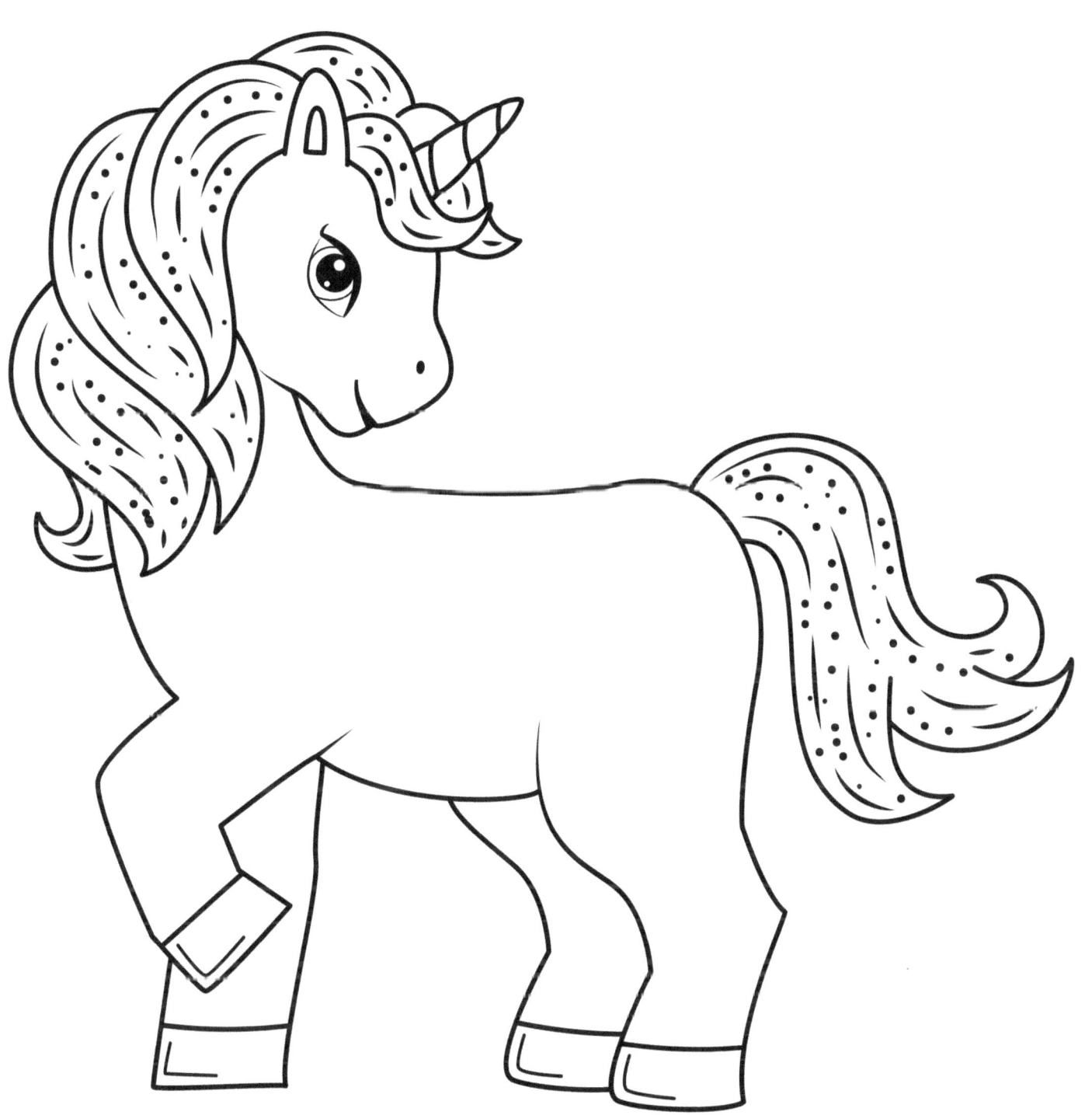

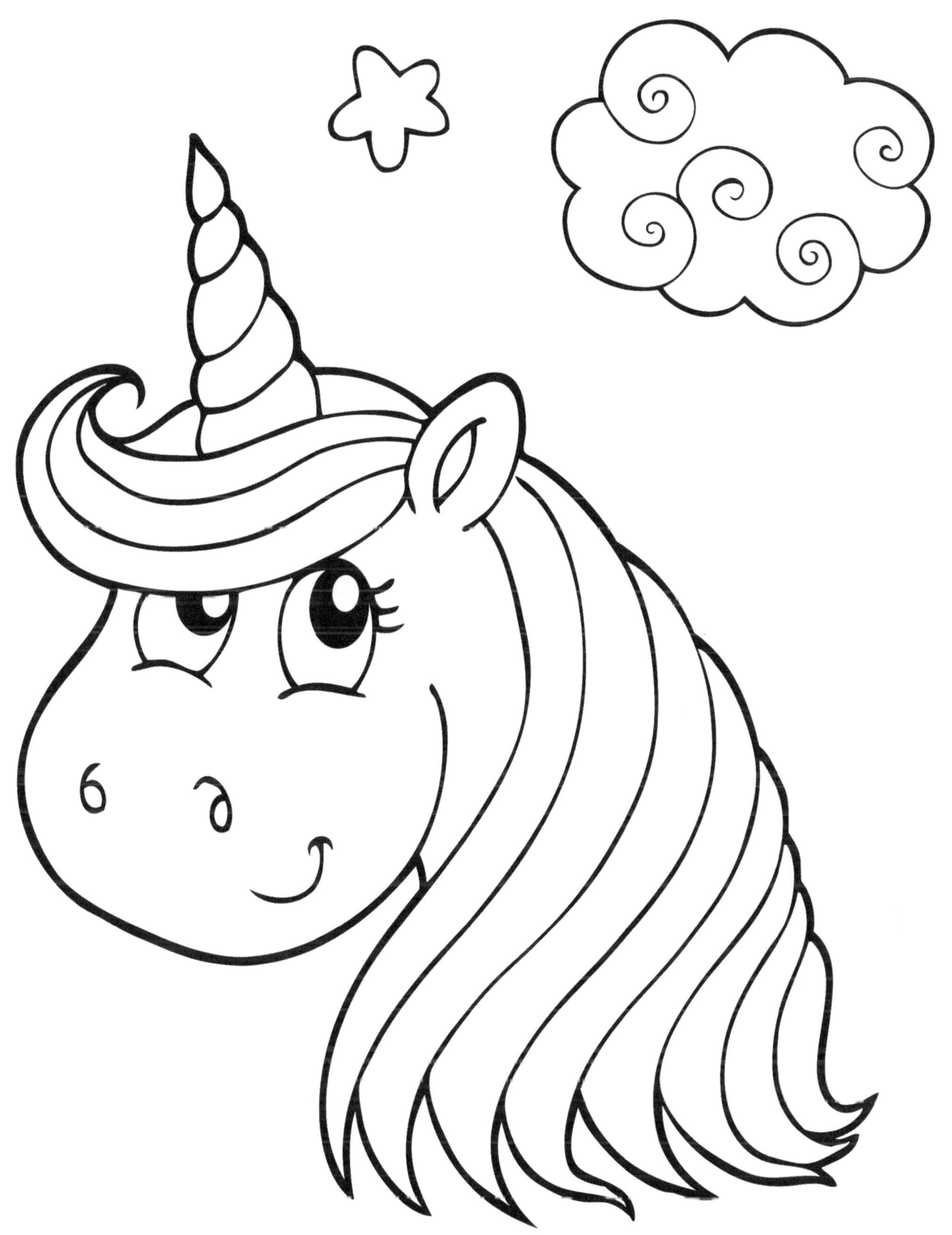

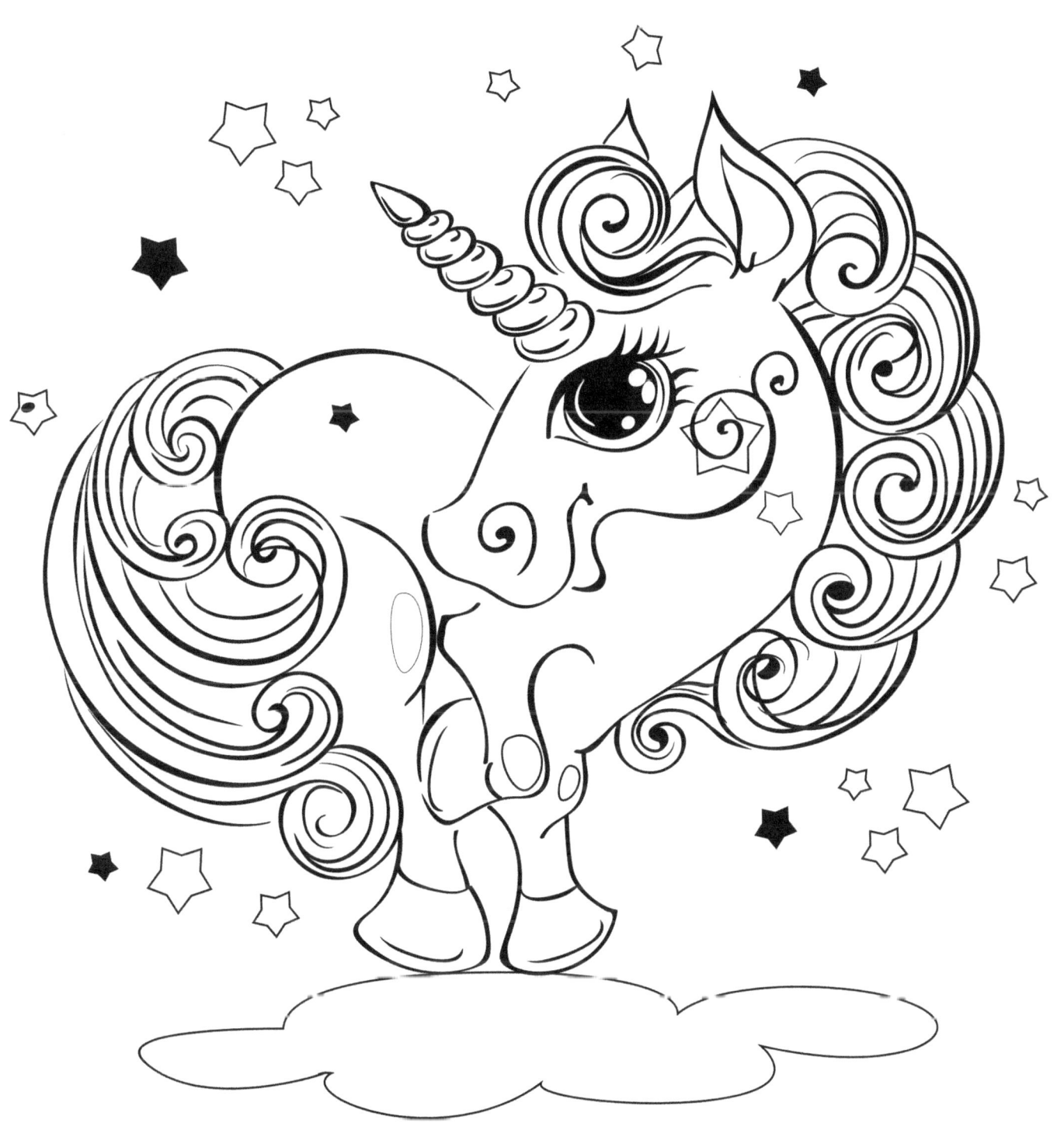